Get Started Fly-Fishing!

Get Started Fly-Fishing!

Craig Schuhmann

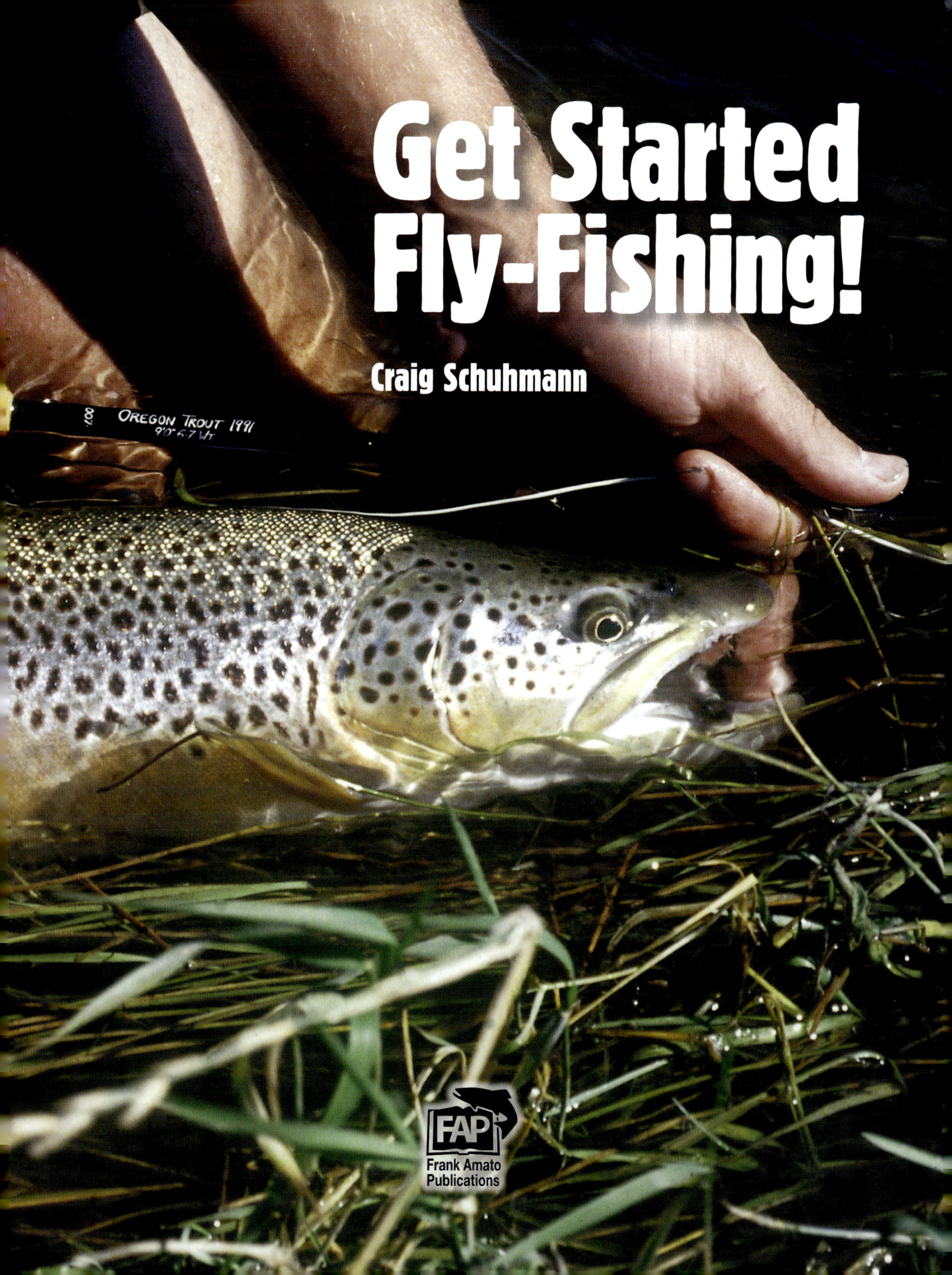

FAP
Frank Amato Publications

For my daughter, Camille Vilasini Schuhmann

Acknowledgements

I'd like to thank Frank Amato for giving me the opportunity to write this book and for all his support and encouragement these past few years. Marlon Rampy, for his beautiful photography and gracious spirit. Dave Hall for his illustrations, artistic spirit, and enthusiasm for the sport. Kim Callahan, Mariah Hinds, and all the staff at Frank Amato Publications for their hard work, encouragement, and patience. Big thanks to Duncan and the crew at Montana Fly Company for supplying samples of their great flies. My dad, Robert N. Schuhmann, and mom Tomette H. Schuhmann, for their constant support and ideas. My students at Klamath Community College whose questions were a constant challenge to improve my teaching. And every angler with whom I have waded through trout waters and shared the mystery of trout.

All inquiries should be addressed to:
Frank Amato Publications, Inc. • P.O. Box 82112 • Portland, Oregon 97282
503-653-8108 • www.AmatoBooks.com

Photography by Marlon Rampy unless otherwise noted
Illustrations by Dave Hall
Fly Plate Photographs by Jim Schollmeyer
Book Design by Mariah Hinds

ISBN-10: 1-57188-473-4
ISBN-13: 978-1-57188-473-2
UPC: 0-81127-00315-0

Printed in Singapore

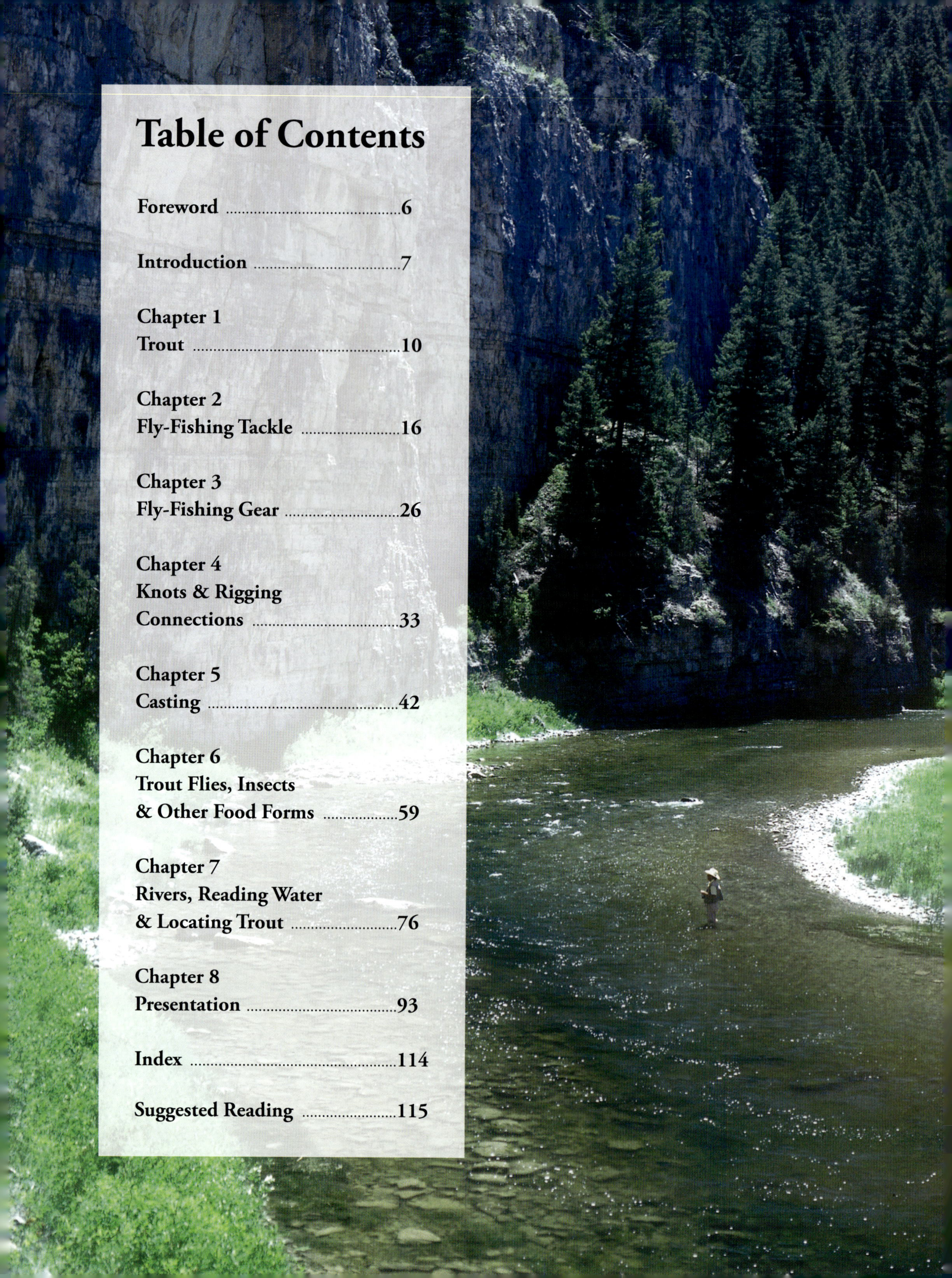

Table of Contents

Foreword

In 1976, publisher Frank Amato received an unsolicited manuscript from a then-unknown author/artist. The book was an introduction to fly-fishing and had been turned down by at least five other publishers. Its author was despairing that it would ever get published.

The book was odd, to say the least: lavishly illustrated, completely hand scrawled, and impulsively humorous. This was the work of an artist gone mad with the pursuit of trout. As Frank would soon learn, the author was even more odd than the book. A mix of beatnik and Renaissance man, he was as likely to be found fishing for trout as scaling the giant granite walls of Yosemite.

Frank was amused and charmed by the book's humor, as well as the articulate and simple lessons it taught. Frank took his chances and published the book without changing a word or illustration, as the author requested. The book, *The Curtis Creek Manifesto* by Sheridan Anderson, is arguably one of the most popular introductions to fly-fishing ever produced, selling well over 300,000 copies to date. Seemingly everyone who has read this book passes it along to future generations of fly-fishers.

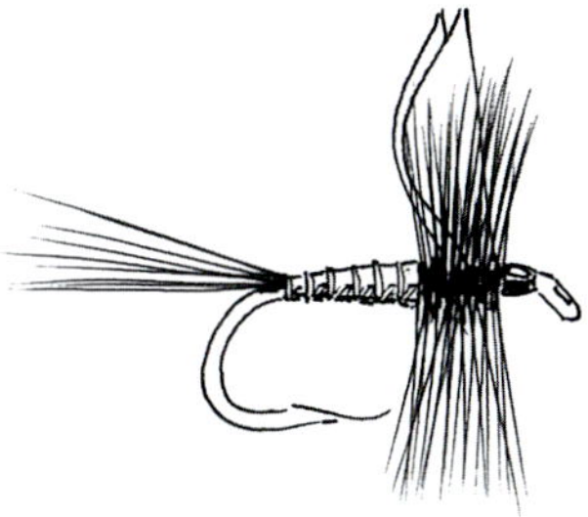

Why is *The Curtis Creek Manifesto* so popular? Part of the reason is the book's humor, but also its simple and readable style. In just 45 pages, half of which are drawings, Sheridan equips his readers with the necessary information to walk up to any stream and catch a trout. Apparently, this type of textbook was sorely needed in its day. As Sheridan says, "The major difficulty with most how-to fishing books is that of trying to figure out what the author is talking about—the beginner is assaulted with page after page of text which he must translate into visual images before he can begin to understand it. Also, most primers fail because they are so overwritten that the novice becomes hopelessly buried under an avalanche of information, much of which is only vaguely incidental to a firm grasp of the basics and thus serving to only confuse the issue." Sheridan labeled such books as Orthodox, "text books which rely too heavily on the printed word."

Few writers will ever hope to compete with the imaginative style, simplicity and grace, not to mention the sales, of *The Curtis Creek Manifesto*. And though it will remain a classic for years to come, there is a time when the old needs to be updated and revised. Fly-fishing is an evolving sport, and while the fundamentals remain unchanged, fishing tactics, equipment and our knowledge of fish and their environment doesn't. The hope of this book is to maintain the spirit of Sheridan's manifesto to "keep it simple" and "visual", but update its contents with contemporary information that today's angler will find helpful.

Introduction

"Despite rumors to the contrary, the paramount objective is: to catch fish."
—Sheridan Anderson, The Curtis Creek Manifesto

This book is specific, an introduction to fly-fishing for trout in rivers. I have intentionally not discussed lake fishing, or fishing for other species such as steelhead, salmon, bass or panfish. I have started at this point because it is where most anglers begin. We start by exploring our home rivers armed with a five-weight fly rod, floating line, and an Adams dry fly, seducing elusive trout from pocket water, riffles, and current seams. This book is designed to help you learn to fly-fish and develop a strategy for approaching a river so you can catch fish. Your task will be to apply this knowledge to a river, either by yourself or with the help of a friend or guide. In addition to this book, there are many ways to learn about fly-fishing and develop your knowledge, and I encourage you to investigate these options. Advanced fly-fishing books, periodicals, internet websites, local and national fly-fishing clubs, friends, and fly shops are just a few of the options.

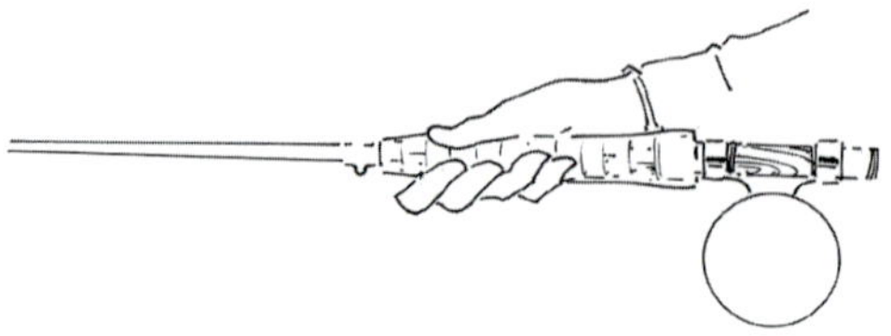

Whenever I teach a basic fly-fishing class, I always begin by comparing traditional methods of fishing (spin and bait-fishing) to fly-fishing. This can make for some lively discussions, especially if there are any spin and bait anglers in the class. Playing the devil's advocate, I always side with these traditional methods, pointing out the obvious benefits: casting is easy and requires little practice, the equipment is simple and inexpensive, one need know only a few knots, and the overall effectiveness of lures and bait is undisputable. If, as Sheridan says, catching fish is the paramount objective of fishing, then the choice should be evident.

So why would anyone choose fly-fishing? The gear is twice as expensive and complicated, with backing, fly lines, leaders, tippet, and an exhausting array of flies and other paraphernalia filling your pockets and covering your vests. Mastering the mechanics of casting and presentation can take several seasons of devoted practice. And the fly-fisherman needs to know at least half a dozen knots.

Needless to say, most students—who signed up for a fly-fishing class, after all—think I've lost my mind. But I'm trying to get each student to think about their choice to pursue fly-fishing.

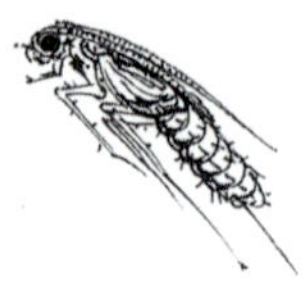

Students want to begin fly-fishing for a variety of reasons. I often hear students say, "Fly-fishing seems more rewarding." Often, this reason comes from traditional anglers seeking new challenges and to avoid messy bait, the use of lead weights or active lures which can deaden the strike and fight of a fish. To these anglers, fly-fishing appears more active, engaging, stimulating, and I think they are right. Fly-fishing gives us a direct, uninhibited connection to the fish.

Some of these anglers are also changing their approach from "catch and keep" to the "catch and release" fishing often advocated among fly-anglers, and flies do have less negative impact on the fish. Without fail, someone always mentions the visual excitement of seeing a fish hit a surface dry fly. That, they tell me, is something spin-anglers do not experience.

Tomette Schuhmann

Still others have reasons which have little to do with fishing and everything to do with the spirit of the sport. Frequently I meet someone for whom fly-fishing holds a connection to their past or to someone who has died. Perhaps a mentor or parent taught them to fly-fish when they were young and they never followed up on the lessons. By far the most common answer to why someone would want to learn to fly-fish is that they love to be in the quiet solitude of mountains and meadows where one often finds rivers and lakes. These students mention fly-fishing as a "purer" approach to catching fish; one that matches the sanctity of the outdoors. Perhaps they like the art of fly-casting or wading in the stream to collect insects. Many students are attracted to the flies themselves, either for their delicate and beautiful construction, or the fact that they resemble the actual food forms trout feed on.

Whatever your reasons for wanting to begin fly-fishing, I can assure you that it is a wonderful and worthwhile journey. It calls on multiple disciplines, is quite thought provoking, and it works for all kinds of people. One need have nothing more than the passion to pursue fish with a fly in order to get started and enjoy fly-angling.

"Catch a Fire"

—Bob Marley

If you are serious about wanting to learn to fly-fish, there is no substitute for time spent on the water. My experiences learning to fly-fish were unique, as yours will be. No two anglers are alike, and, depending upon where you fish, your challenges will be unique to the waters you fish and the species you are after. Generalized fishing techniques are important to learn, but expect most of your learning to come from the particular requirements of the waters you choose to fish.

There is an understanding born out of the collective experience of anglers that one must put in their time before they start to catch fish consistently. This was true for me, and you can expect it to be true for you. However, the day will come, as it does for all anglers, when learning pays off and we begin to experience the sport from the inside, as participants and co-creators with our inherited fly-fishing traditions. My goal for you is nothing short of this kind of transcendent experience and all-consuming joy that I find in fly-fishing.

While the purpose of fishing may be to catch fish, I hope you will come to enjoy the simple activity of fishing, as I do. I imagine that there is very little difference between the satisfaction gained from a day spent fishing and a day playing golf, skiing, or building model airplanes. All are immersions into something which presents a challenge, tests our skills, and connects us to the larger world. That which defines a successful angler will vary in definition from

person to person, but one thing is certain: fishing is a sport about which we will never have all the answers, and in that way remains an inviting mystery.

I am fond of the saying "confidence catches fish." This says nothing about the gear we use, the types of flies we choose, or the way we present a fly, although these things are important.

By reading this book and applying its principles, you will have some of the answers which demystify trout and rivers and have the confidence that you can catch fish.

"There is a fire in water"

—David James Duncan

1

Trout

"If Fishing were simply a matter of catching Fish or forming and testing angling theories, I think I should have given it up long ago. Nor is it simply a matter of exciting and beautiful surroundings, the splendor and loveliness of running water and the attraction that rivers have for creatures of all kinds, including Man. These are a large and important part of it all, but one can enjoy them without going Fishing and I often do. I think perhaps the lasting charm of Fishing is in the pace of the sport and in the Fish themselves."

—Roderick Haig-Brown,
Fisherman's Fall (1964)

Prior to the mid-1800's, trout lived exclusively in their native rivers and lakes. Thus, if one wanted to catch brown trout, Europe would be your destination; brook trout could be found only in northeastern North America; and rainbow, cutthroat and bull trout inhabited the rivers and lakes of the Pacific slope of North America. With a few exceptions, trout did not exist outside these regions.

By the late 1800's trout went global with the invention of fish hatcheries. Fish-stocking practices allowed trout to inhabit non-native waters all over the world, and as far south as New Zealand, South Africa, and South America.

Not all trout are the same and in this chapter we will look at five of the most popular species: rainbow, cutthroat, brown, brook, and bull trout. This information will help you identify the type of trout you may be catching in your home waters and offer clues about how to approach these different fish. We will note each trout's distinctive appearance, and identify a few characteristics, preferences, and subspecies.

Rainbow Trout

Rainbow trout (*Oncorhynchus mykiss*)* are native to the pacific slope of North America ranging from Alaska to Mexico; as far east as Montana, Wyoming, Colorado and New Mexico; with minor populations existing across the Bering Straight in Asia. From the west coast of North America they have been transplanted all over the world wherever cold waters exist and are arguably the most popular and widely dispersed trout in the world. Rainbows are known for

Rainbow Trout

* Scientific names indicate a) genus and b) species.

their fight, propensity to feed on stages of aquatic insects and as a great eating fish.

The name 'rainbow' derives from their iridescent coloration, most notably the red or pink rainbow stripe on silvery sides. There are two types of rainbow trout, the coastal and redband. Redbands can be distinguished from coastal rainbows by their pronounced brick-red sides. Numerous subspecies exist within these two types and each is distinguished by variations in color and locations in different watersheds.

Both coastal and redband rainbows may be resident-stream types or anadromous (ocean-going). Resident rainbows spend their whole life cycle in a freshwater river, spawning in the spring. Anadromous rainbows, called steelhead, migrate to the ocean and return to fresh water to spawn in either the summer or winter.

The average size of a rainbow is 6-8 inches in small streams and 12-16 inches or larger in bigger rivers and lakes. Steelhead average 18-30 inches and can reach over 40 inches. Most trout can live 3-7 years depending on environmental factors and steelhead live 4-7 years.

Both coastal and redband rainbows may be resident-stream types or anadromous (ocean-going).

Steelhead average 18-30 inches and can reach over 40 inches.

Cutthroat Trout

Cutthroat trout (*Oncorhynchus clarki*) are also native to western North America and share the same geographical region as the rainbow trout. Cutthroat trout are not as widespread as rainbows and tend to be isolated in particular regions. Cutthroat exhibit a much wider diversity of species than do rainbow trout and many of these differences are traced to particular watersheds. Altogether there are 14 different species of cutthroat trout, examples include the coastal, westslope, Yellowstone, Snake River fine-spotted, greenback and Lahontan. The coastal cutthroat is the only anadromous species, spending two or three months of its lifecycle in the shallows and inland areas and estuaries of the Pacific Ocean, returning to fresh water in the fall.

Generally, cutthroats may be distinguished from rainbows in two ways: the presence of red or orange colored slash marks on the outside of the lower jaw and the absence of a pronounced red or pink band of

Cutthroat exhibit a much wider diversity of species than do rainbow trout and many of these differences are traced to particular watersheds. Altogether there are 14 different species of cutthroat trout.

Cutthroat Trout

color on its flanks. However, these are somewhat unreliable identifiers since some rainbows also share these visual markings. The problem of identification can be further compounded by crossbreeding of the species. Many species of cutthroat tend towards a yellow hue and a reduced number of spots particularly across the top of the head and front sides.

Cutthroat are spring spawners and average 6-8 inches in small rivers and 16-18 inches in larger rivers and lakes. Typical lifespan is same as a rainbow's, 3-7 years depending on environmental factors.

Brown Trout

Brown trout are a close relative to the Atlantic salmon.

Brown trout (*Salmo trutta*) is the species that brought about the birth of fly-angling, when our sport was invented in the British Isles in the sixteenth century. Brown trout are a close relative to the Atlantic salmon, native to British Isles and Europe and were introduced into America in the 1880's. Since that time brown trout have been transplanted with great success all over the world. America has viewed this fish with mixed emotions, ranging from disdain to admiration. The current popularity of brown trout may be mixed, but there is no argument that this is one of the most challenging trout to catch.

Brown Trout

Brown trout are unique, behaviorally, from native rainbows, cutthroats and brook trout. Angling lore has portrayed the brown trout as an elusive, predator fish, with selective feeding habits. In fact, brown trout have a few characteristic that make them attractive to fly-anglers, namely, their ability to survive in warm waters and their propensity to feed on aquatic insects, particularly dry flies.

In larger streams which support populations of baitfish, crayfish, and terrestrial populations of grasshoppers, frogs and even mice, the brown trout is known to feed exclusively on these larger food forms. As streamer-fishermen know, browns can be quite aggressive chasing

Brown trout, like this one, can be the most challenging fish to catch in a river. Brent Hublitz

down big wet flies. Brown trout prefer protected areas in a river, such as rocks, logs, shaded areas and undercut banks, and are known to station themselves in these areas.

With some allowances for variation in color, brown trout are easily identified from other types of trout with a profusion of black and red spots on a brown yellowish body. To help you distinguish brown trout from most char such as brook and bull trout, think "light background, dark spots." A reliable identifier is the absence of any spots on the tail (caudal) fin.

Brown trout average 10-12 inches in smaller streams and 14-30 inches in larger rivers and lakes. Browns typically spawn in the fall. Browns have a longer average lifespan than most trout and can live from 5-12 years or more.

In larger streams which support populations of baitfish, crayfish, and terrestrial populations of grasshoppers, frogs and even mice, the brown trout is known to feed exclusively on these larger food forms.

Brook Trout

Native to northeastern North America, the brook trout was the mainstay of East Coast fly-angling traditions until the introduction of brown and rainbow trout in the late 1800's.

Brook trout (*Salvelinus fontinalis*) are the trout on which America began its fly-fishing traditions when the sport was first imported from the British Isles in the late 1700's. Native to northeastern North America, the brook trout was the mainstay of East Coast fly-angling traditions until the introduction of brown and rainbow trout in the late 1800's. These later species were perceived by many as a welcomed introduction, offering more challenging sport than the often gullible brook trout. Today, brook trout enjoy a loyal following of anglers all over the world who appreciate what may be the most beautiful of trout.

Brook trout, along with lake trout, bull trout, arctic char, and Dolly Varden are known as char. Chars are distinct from rainbow, cutthroat, and brown trout by their absence of black spots. Instead, the spotting is hued in lighter tones, such as pink, yellow, red, and cream, all set against a dark olive or gray background. The backs of brook trout are mottled with striking worm-like venations.

Brook trout have been naturalized throughout most of the United States and all over the world. Like most chars, brook trout prefer cold water well below what other trout prefer, but are tolerant of warmer water. Brook trout actively feed on insects and come readily to a dry fly, nymph, or streamer.

Brook trout average 4-5 inches in small cold creeks and can reach six pounds or more in lakes and larger rivers. Brook trout are fall spawners and live relatively short lives of 2-3 years depending on environmental factors.

Brook Trout

Bull Trout

Bull trout (*Salvelinus confluentus*), also a member of the char family, are native to colder rivers in western North America from British Columbia to Oregon and east to Montana and Idaho. Bull trout have been listed as a threatened species since 1998 and are currently found in Canada and five U.S. states: Oregon, Washington, Montana, Idaho, and Alaska. Fishing for bull trout is often off limits, but does exist in a few places, so read your regulations carefully.

Bull trout have long been confused with Dolly Varden, but scientific evidence has shown them to be a distinct species. Bull trout are not always easily identified because they can have spotting and body color similar to lake trout, brook trout and brown trout. Bull trout have grayish bodies with small white, yellow, and red or pink spots. One positive identification marker of a bull trout is a black fin with the absence of any spotting.

When fishing in waters containing bull trout, anglers have to be extra cautious about not confusing this fish with other species. Thus, the slogan "fin black, put it back" is a helpful reminder for anglers needing to identify a bull trout.

Bull trout hold in deeper waters at the bottom of pools where the water is cooler. They require clean, cool river drainages which is part of the reason for their threatened species status; many of our rivers are suffering from habitat loss and deterioration which threatens their survivability. Even the young stay on the bottom of the river feeding on invertebrates and do not start feeding on the surface like other trout. Bull trout are opportunistic feeders. Large fish tend to feed exclusively on other fish (piscivorous).

Bull trout average 8-10 inches in smaller streams and 28-36 inches in larger rivers and lakes. Bull trout spawn in the fall, migrating to small streams and tributaries of their parent river or lake.

When fishing in waters containing bull trout, anglers have to be extra cautious about not confusing this fish with other species. Thus, the slogan "fin black, put it back" is a helpful reminder for anglers needing to identify a bull trout.

Bull Trout

2

Fly-Fishing Tackle

The best way to begin is to walk into your local fly shop and ask if you can cast a few demo rods and reels.

When buying a starter outfit for trout fishing in rivers, I recommend paying $100-$250 for a graphite rod, $100-$150 for a machined bar-stock aluminum large-arbor reel, and $60 for a weight-forward floating fly line.

Having the right gear is important, so it pays to research which equipment is best for you. Too often I see anglers struggling with problems such as casting, presentation or hooking and landing a fish—all of which are related to equipment. This is particularly common with intermediate-level anglers who are still using starter-level rods, reels and lines. These same anglers often excel in ways they didn't think was possible when taught to use more advanced equipment.

The three variables to consider when deciding which gear to purchase are: budget, skill level, and type of fishing. When buying a starter outfit for trout fishing in rivers, I recommend paying $100-$250 for a graphite rod, $100-$150 for a machined bar-stock aluminum large-arbor reel, and $60 for a weight-forward floating fly line. At the low end, that's $260 for a basic set-up. In this budget range you can expect to get an outfit you may never outgrow. Cheaper equipment comes with the cost of having to buy new equipment once your skill level increases. If you can afford more expensive equipment, then I say go for it. Avoid buying prepackaged kits (rod, reel, line combinations) which will have little value past the beginning stages of learning.

Go with established fly-fishing-only brand names such as Sage, Winston, Thomas & Thomas, Orvis, Temple Fork Outfitters, Echo, Rio, Scientific Anglers and Airflow to get good reliability and warranties. You will break a few rods, smash a few reels and damage a few lines, so it's nice to know that all of the above manufacturers will replace or repair your gear for a small service fee.

If you already own your own equipment, then great! It can be used to practice all the principles in this book. If you need to buy equipment, don't buy anything you can't test first. The best way to begin is to walk into your local fly shop and ask if you can cast a few demo rods and reels. Let the sales person know your skill level and the type of fishing you're doing and they will guide you through the process of selecting the best rod and reel for you. Fly shop sales people are often experienced casters themselves, and this is not a bad way to get a quick casting lesson.

Don't make a decision until after you have cast a few rods and, even then, you may want to try some different brands at another shop. Your decision about which rod and reel to buy is going to be based on comfort, what feels the best, and what you can afford. The rest of this chapter will educate you on the basic equipment and give you some guidelines about what to look for when purchasing modern fly-fishing equipment for trout fishing.

Fly-Rod Outfit

The basic fly-rod outfit is composed of a rod, reel and fly line. Fly-fishing outfits come in various weights, designated by numbers #1 through #12 and higher. The term "weight" is an industry measurement related to performance, not the physical weight of the equipment. When the rod, line and reel are matched to the same weight they are said to be "balanced" and will offer optimum performance. Thus, a five-weight rod is best matched with a five-weight line and reel.

The weight of the outfit is selected according to the type of fish you're pursuing, plus a few other factors such as size of flies, type of water, and casting conditions like wind and back-casting room. A one-weight is the lightest possible outfit, and something of a novelty, used on very small fish and equally small rivers. A 12-weight is used for saltwater fishing and for larger game such as salmon. A five- or six-weight is the perfect all-around outfit for most trout fishing conditions.

The weight of the outfit is selected according to the type of fish you're pursuing, plus a few other factors such as size of flies, type of water, and casting conditions like wind and back-casting room.

Fly Rods

Rod Material

Fly rods are constructed for casting performance, and the most important attributes are physical weight, flex or action, and durability. All these factors are determined by the type of material used and the specific rod maker. The best rod-building material today is graphite, a carbon-fiber material first developed in the military and used in many products such as golf shafts, tent poles, and skis. Compared to traditional rod-making materials such as wood, bamboo and fiberglass, graphite is a more versatile material that allows rod makers to construct durable, lightweight rods of varying flex or action.

Rod Action

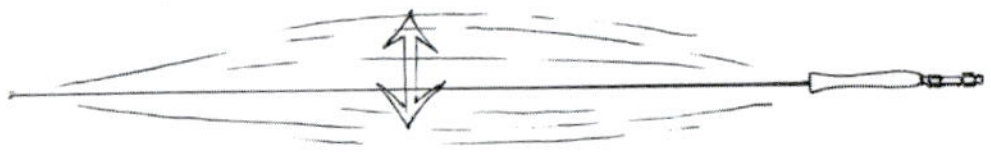

Fast Action

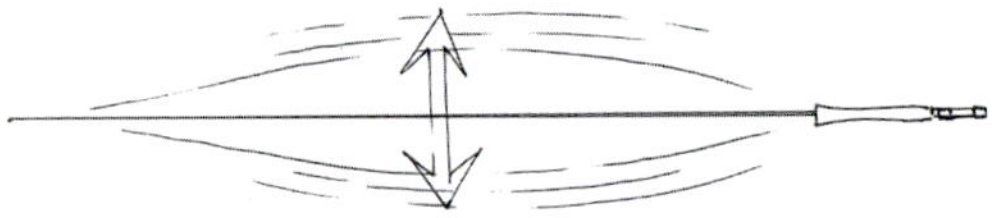

Medium Action

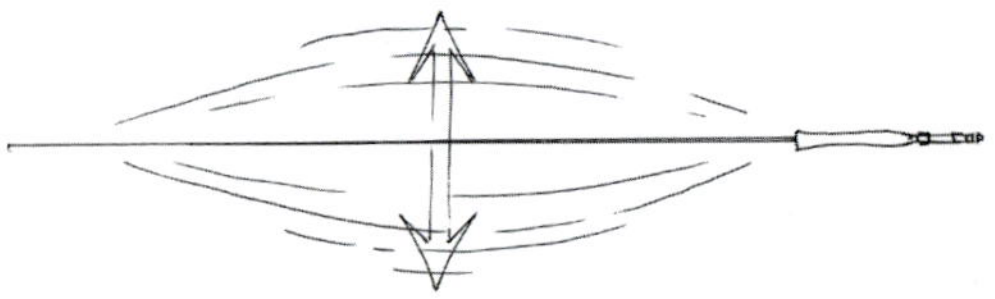

Slow Action

Rod Action

Your decision on which action or flex is best for you will, in part, be based on the type of fishing you do, and also on your abilities. Rod action or flex is defined as how the rod loads under the pressure of casting and the weight of the first 30 feet of fly line. In other words, flex refers to where the rod carries the load of the fly line when it is cast: either at the tip, through the middle of the rod or near the butt-section.

The flex of the rod is determined by the type of material it is made of and the design of the taper. All rods are constructed with a taper which progresses from a small-diameter tip to a larger diameter butt section. A rod that carries the load of casting into the butt section is said to be a slow-action rod, meaning it takes longer for the rod to load before it can be recast. A rod that loads in the middle is a medium-action rod, and a rod that loads at the tip is fast action.

Progressive-action rods, a fairly new development in rod making, have a soft tip and a stiff butt section and are designed to distribute the load of the cast uniformly through the rod. Progressive-action rods are generally considered medium to medium-fast action and are a good rod for the beginner. When in doubt, go with a faster-action rod. They will handle the delicate presentation needed for dry-fly fishing and still able to throw weighted nymphs and streamers.

Rod action or flex is defined as how the rod loads under the pressure of casting and the weight of the first 30 feet of fly line.

Rod Outfit

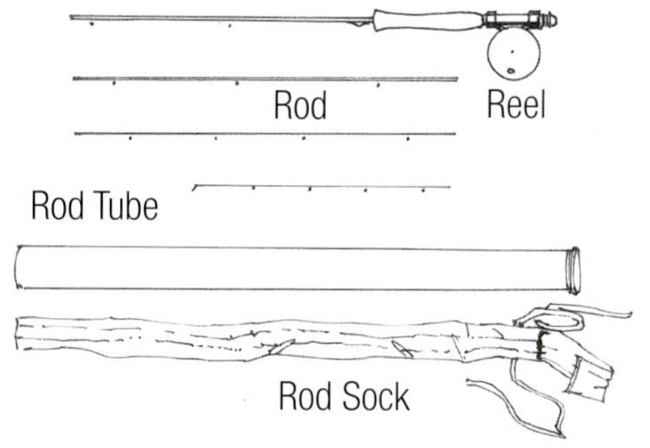

Rod Length and Pieces

Rods come in various lengths and number of pieces. Rod lengths range from a short 6 1/2 feet to 10 feet and longer. The most common range for most beginning anglers is 8 1/2 to 9 feet. This length will allow for a good range of casting distances, mending ability (which will be discussed below), and leverage when playing a fish—the three most important features of rod length. Shorter rods of 6 1/2 to 7 1/2 feet are good for smaller rivers or streams when distance casting is not required and back-casting is limited. Longer rods over 9 feet are good for lakes, especially when casting from a belly boat or pontoon boat, and for larger rod weights, such as a 10- or 12-weight, when catching bigger game.

Rods also come in different piece configurations: one, two, three, and four or more. Most rods today come in four pieces or sections which are then fitted together to form the entire rod. Ten to 15 years ago, most rods were two-piece. Part of this trend towards four-piece rods is portability; four-piece rods are easier to travel with and store. There have also been improvements in rod-building materials which allow for more sections without the loss of performance.

Rod Components

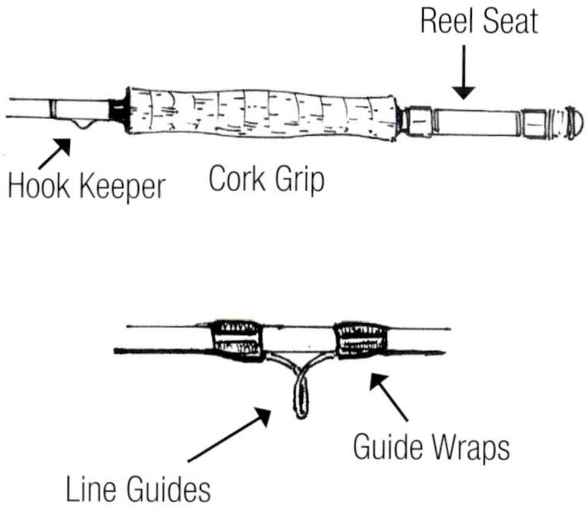

Rod Components

All rods come equipped with a standard set of components: guides, grip, reel seat, and hook keep. Guides are the small loops or rings strategically spaced along one side of the rod shaft that allow the line to be projected in a straight line. The grip, most often made of cork, is where the angler holds the rod when casting. The reel seat, located on the bottom of the rod below the grip, is where the reel attaches to the rod. And the hook keep sits near the reel and stores the hook when not in use. All these features are important to the overall performance of the rod but need not be considered in-depth when making a purchase. The most important considerations are that the grip feels comfortable in your hand, the reel seat holds the reel securely in place without coming loose, and the line shoots straight out the guides. Be aware that many rod makers will embellish these components with higher priced materials making rods more expensive.

The most important considerations are that the grip feels comfortable in your hand, the reel seat holds the reel securely in place without coming loose, and the line shoots straight out the guides.

Fly Reels

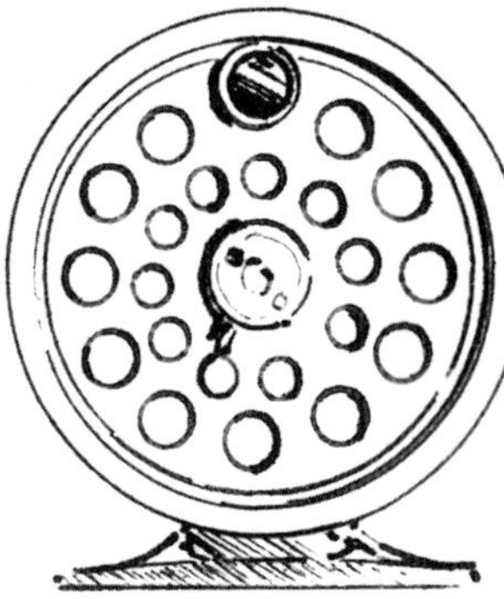

Fly Reel

Reels house the components of fly-line backing, fly line, and leader, but can also function to balance the casting action of your rod. It may be the simplest component of your fly-rod outfit, and the decision about what kind of reel to buy will rest on a few basic requirements: the reel should match the type of rod you're using, be constructed of a durable material, should retrieve the line easily and smoothly, and include some kind of drag mechanism. I suggest that you consider investing a little money in a reel ($100 or more) and not go with the cheapest available. Nothing is worse than having a great rod with a dumpy reel. As any experienced angler will tell you, reels do more than just hold line. Reels are performance items, and we constantly rely on them when it comes to playing fish, stripping off line to make a cast, or making a fast retrieve to put line back on your reel.

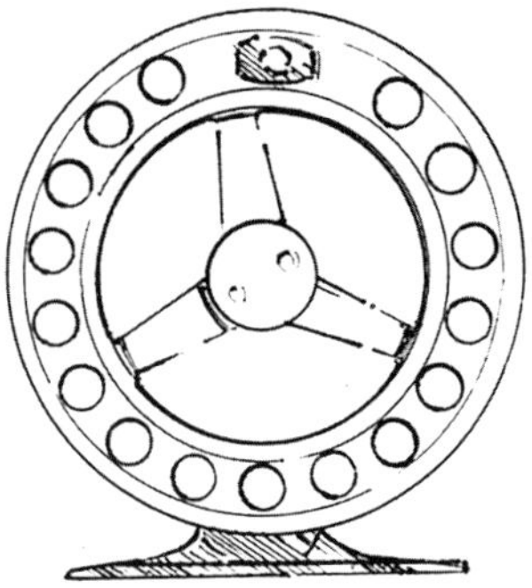

Large-Arbor Reel

Reels have two parts: the housing and spool. The spool turns in the housing and holds the fly line. The housing contains the drag system and anchor or footing, which attaches to the rod. Spools can be removed from the housing either for cleaning or to attach another spool with different fly line. Depending on your type of fishing, you may want to purchase an extra spool for different fly lines. Choose a reel with a spool that comes with an easy-release mechanism.

When considering a reel you will have to choose between a large, medium or standard-arbor, referring to the diameter of the center of the spool. The trend today is for large- and medium-arbor reels. These larger-arbor reels offer a couple of benefits over standard arbors: they retrieve more line with fewer turns of the spool, and they do not spool the line as tightly, allowing it to be pulled off the reel easier and with less resistance. Most manufacturers have moved away from standard-arbor reels in favor of large arbors, so chances are you will be buying a large arbor, even in the low-priced reels.

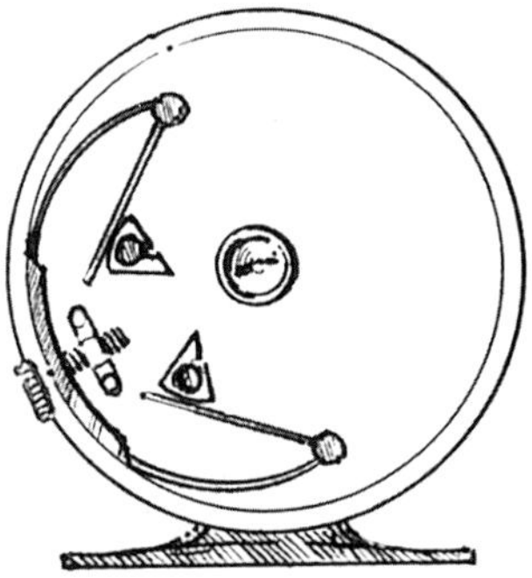

Click and Pawl Drag

Most reels come with a drag mechanism which applies pressure to the spool and keeps it from over-spinning your line. A good drag system is particularly important when playing bigger fish which have a tendency to run fast and hard and can backlash your reel causing the fish to break-off. Drag systems come in two types: click and pawl, and disk. The former sets only minor drag to the spool and is found mostly on smaller reels where it is assumed smaller fish are being caught. Disk drags can be set to apply a lot of pressure to line being pulled off the reel and are used primarily on larger reels, for larger game such as salmon, steelhead and large trout. Many five-weight reels also come with disk drags, this can be a good feature if you are catching larger fish, but it will increase the price of the reel.

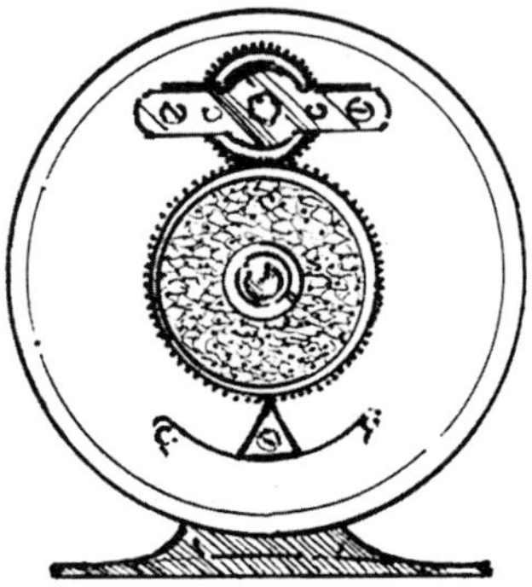

Disk Drag

Reels are made with a variety of materials, such as die-cast aluminum, machined solid bar-stock aluminum and carbon fiber plastic. Die-cast aluminum is found on less expensive reels and tends to be clunky and less durable. Machined solid bar-stock aluminum reels are machined from a single piece of aluminum and are very tight fitting, smooth running, durable and corrosion resistant. Bar-stock reels are the tools of choice for most anglers but can cost two to three times the money. Carbon fiber plastic reels are becoming more popular because they can offer the benefits of a large arbor with cheaper material that is both durable and corrosion resistant. Carbon fiber reels are relatively new to the market, so durability and performance over time have yet to be proven when compared with aluminum reels.

Fly Lines

Ted Lesson, in his book *The Habit of Rivers*, has surmised that all aspects of our sport, including equipment, can be deduced from the fly. In essence, he argues that we can reconstruct all the equipment needed to deliver a small speck of material, weighing nothing, long distances in a delicate manner. This trick is largely accomplished by the nature and design of a fly line, combined with the casting motion of the rod. Unlike in spin-fishing, where the weight of the lure pulls the line off the reel, fly-fishing relies on the weight of the line to deliver a fly.

Fly lines come in two basic shapes, double taper and weight forward, and a variety of colors. Most fly lines used for trout have a length up to 90 feet and are composed of a front tip, front taper, body, rear taper, and rear tip or running line. Double-taper lines have a symmetrical shape with a thick body, and an equal length of taper and tip in the front and rear. Double-tapers are a traditional style line preferred by anglers whose fishing styles require shorter casts. Some casting techniques, such as mending, roll casts, and delicate presentations, are easier with double-taper lines. Double-taper lines are considered more economical because when one end wears, you can flip it over and use the other end.

Weight-forward lines are tapered so that the weight of the line is compressed in the first 30 feet of fly line, making the front of the line thicker and heavier, and the remainder of the line thinner. Weight-forward lines have replaced double-taper lines as the standard primarily because they are easier to cast and they work better with faster-action rods. Double-taper lines are good all-around lines and allow longer casts with greater ease. Opinions about which line to buy varies depending upon angler preference and style of fishing. I recommend a weight-forward line for all your fishing simply because they are easier to cast.

The line color you choose is personal preference and your options run from bright fluorescent to muted earth tones or white. Part of the decision about color concerns are theories about what the trout can see. Muted colors would seem to attract less attention from the fish than bright-colored lines, but they can be harder for the angler to see on the water. I suggest muted colors for clear, smooth rivers

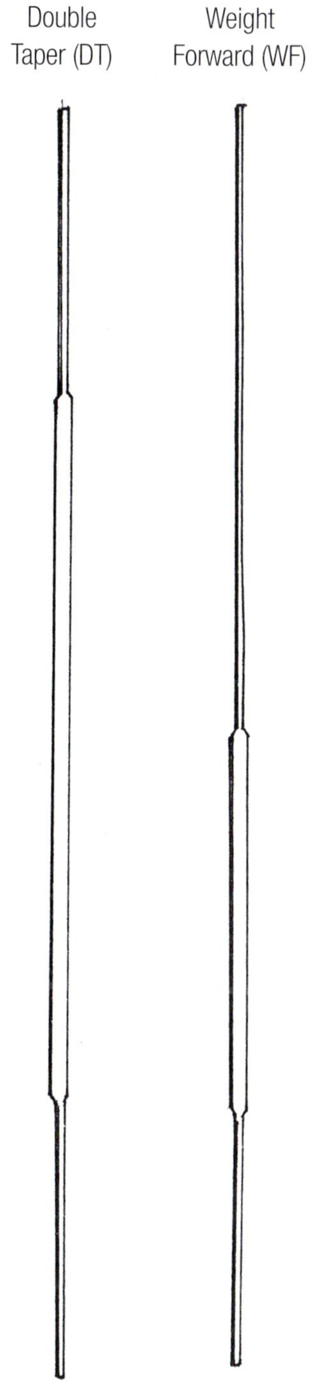

Types of Fly Lines

Weight-forward lines utilize only one end of the fly line whereas double-taper lines can be flipped around to utilize both ends when one end wears out.

such as spring creeks and brighter colors for faster rivers and broken water. If you only buy one line then go with what is least offensive to your senses and you'll be safe.

Beginning anglers fishing for trout in rivers need only one line to begin.

Beginning anglers fishing for trout in rivers need only one line to begin, whether it is a weight forward or double taper. This line will enable you to fish dry flies, nymphs and streamers. There are many lines on the market, including specialty tapers designed for specific fishing conditions, and you may want to explore some of these as your ability improves. In addition to floating lines there are full-sinking and sink-tip lines. These are high-density lines, smaller in diameter than floating lines, which incorporate sinking materials such as lead, in their construction. Full-sinking lines sink over their entire length after breaking the water surface. Sink-tip lines have a sinking tip backed by floating line. Sinking or sink-tip lines are useful when fishing streamers or fishing on lakes. Full-sinking and sink-tip lines come in various sink rates calculated by the number of inches they sink per second. A slow-sinking line, also called an intermediate line, may sink .5-.75 inches per second; a fast-sinking line sinks anywhere from 6-8 inches per second.

Full-sinking and sink-tip lines come in various sink rates calculated by the number of inches they sink per second.

Leaders and Tippet

A fly-rod outfit is completed by the addition of a clear monofilament tapered leader, with your fly line knotted to one end and the fly tied to the other. Leaders and tippets have several uses, and their importance cannot be overestimated (see Chapter 8: Presentation, page 89). Poorly constructed or inappropriate leaders can cause many problems related to presentation and casting that are easily overcome by selecting the correct leader. First, it would not be possible to attach a fly to the end of a thick fly line. Second, a leader separates the fly from the colored fly line which can potentially spook fish. And third, leaders are designed to cast the fly efficiently and give the fly a natural appearance in the water. Leaders, in effect, act as a cushion between fly line and fly, allowing the fly to drift naturally on the water currents.

Leaders and tippets have several uses, and their importance cannot be overestimated.

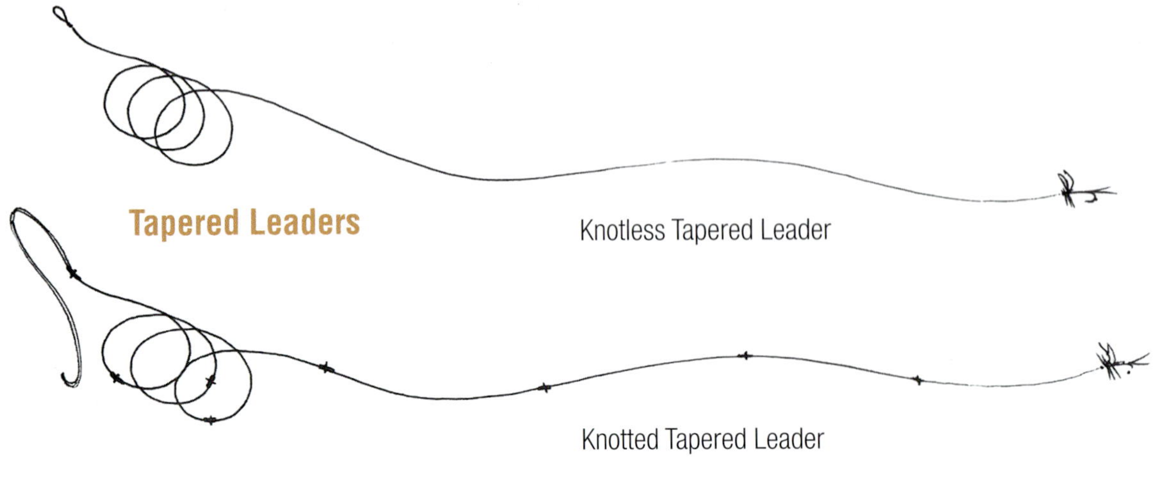

Tapered Leaders

Tippet to Fly Sizes

Tippet Diameter	Pound Test*	Hook Size
.011 (0X)	10 (16.5)	1/0-4
.010 (1X)	8.5 (14.5)	4-8
.009 (2X)	7 (12.5)	6-10
.008 (3X)	6 (9.2)	10-14
.007 (4X)	5 (7.0)	12-16
.006 (5X)	4 (4.8)	14-22
.005 (6X)	3 (3.7)	16-24
.004 (7X)	2 (2.6)	18-22
.003 (8X)	1.2 (1.9)	22-smaller

*Bracketed numbers under Pound Test are for fluorocarbon.

Anglers have the option of two types of leader/tippet material: monofilament and fluorocarbon. Monofilament is the standard for most fishing situations and has been for years. The use of fluorocarbon is a hotly debated issue among anglers primarily because it costs twice as much as monofilament. But fluorocarbon does have proven advantages over monofilament. The primary advantages are that it is less visible to fish, sinks faster, has greater strength in smaller diameters and is more durable. Fluorocarbon will also last through several seasons because it is not susceptible to breakdown from exposure to UV light.

Not all fishing situations demand fluorocarbon, and its benefits are predicated on our theories about how fish see and respond to leaders and tippet material, but it does seem to have an advantage when fishing rivers such as clear water, or heavily fished waters where leader-shy fish may pose a problem.

Leaders are measured in length and tippet strength, with the tippet being the last two feet of tapered leader. A 9-foot, 4x leader would be a 9-foot-long leader with a tippet of approximately 5-pound test. Leaders come in various lengths from 5-15 feet with tippet strengths from 7x (2-pound test) to 0x (12-pound test).

The construction of tapered leaders begins with a thick-diameter butt section of 15-pound test or more and reduces gradually to a small-diameter tip. The tapered design of the leader continues the taper of the fly line, allowing an efficient transfer of energy in the cast to allow the line to lie straight out in front of you without bunching up on the water. A 9-foot leader is a good all-purpose leader for trout. Tippet size will depend on the size of fly you're using (see chart).

Leaders come in two forms: knotted or knotless. Knotted leaders can be purchased commercially or tied by hand using varying diameter tippets and a leader formula. The main drawback of knotted leaders is the knots, which seem to catch every bit of vegetation in the river and require constant cleaning. Knotless leaders solve this problem and are the preferred choice of most anglers. The complaint with

The tapered design of the leader continues the taper of the fly line, allowing an efficient transfer of energy in the cast to allow the line to lie straight out in front of you without bunching up on the water.

Leaders come in two forms: knotted or knotless.

Recommendations for the Starting Outfit

9-foot, 5- to 6-weight medium/fast-action fly rod (9' 5-6-weight)

5- to 6-weight large-arbor solid bar-stock machined aluminum reel

5- to 6-weight, weight-forward floating line (WF-F-5)

9' 4x tapered leader

Tippet spools in 3x, 4x, 5x, 6x

Reel backing: Recommended quantity of Dacron backing

Consider your tippet size when choosing which size of fly to use.

most knotless leaders is they are only available commercially, so one has to rely on the tapered design set by the manufacturer. Many anglers who buy knotless leaders feel the necessity to alter the design by either removing butt material or attaching extra tippet.

The tippet, the last two feet of tapered leader, consists of a single-diameter material. Tippets get reduced as you add and remove flies or encounter break-offs. So, most anglers will carry several spools of different-diameter tippet to attach to the leader as needed.

Tippet sizes are designated by an "x" system and are measured in diameters and breaking strength, called pound test (see chart). Tippet sizes are not standardized and vary according to manufacturer and the type of material being used. Fluorocarbon, for instance, has greater breaking strength with smaller diameters. Thus, a better way to select size tippets is by looking at the diameter of material rather than relying on the "x" system. Generally, one selects a tippet size or tippet diameter according to the size of fly being used (see chart page 23).

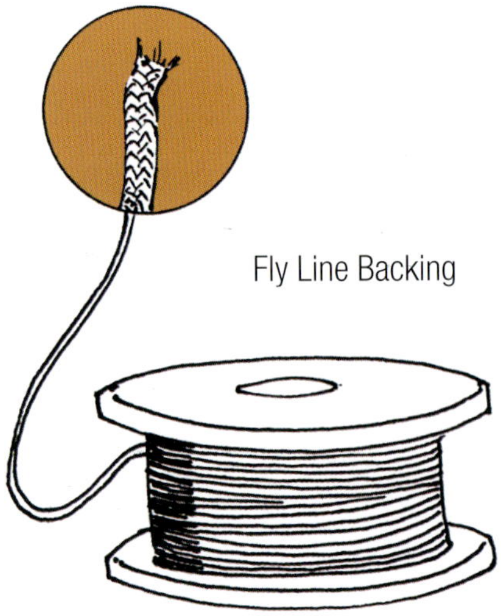

Fly-Line Backing

The first thing to be spooled onto your reel is fly-line backing, a braided Dacron material that extends the length of your fly line. Fly lines are only 90 feet, and a hard-running fish might strip all the fly line off your reel. With 100 feet or more of backing you save both fish and fly line. The capacity of your reel as set by the manufacturer will include both fly line and backing. Backing also has the effect of increasing the diameter of your reel, thus storing your line with less kinks and making it easier to come off the reel smoothly.

Weight-forward lines are designed to help you make longer casts.

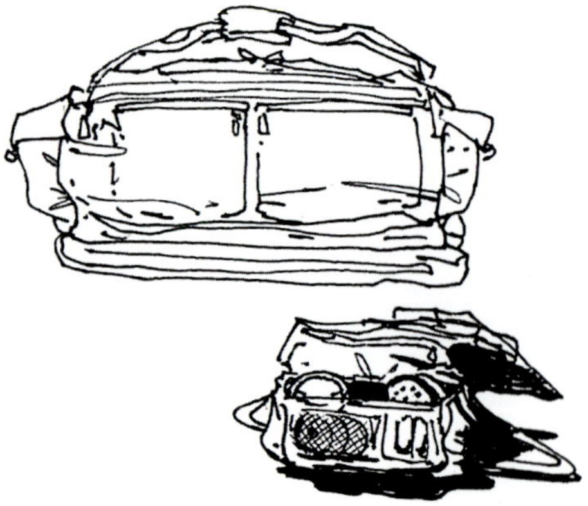

Gear and Tackle Bag

Select a gear bag with a separate compartment to store wet waders and boots away from dry clothing, net, wading staff, and fishing vest or chest pack. A second gear bag or boat bag holds all your fishing gear such as reels, fly boxes, tippet spools and other fishing accessories.

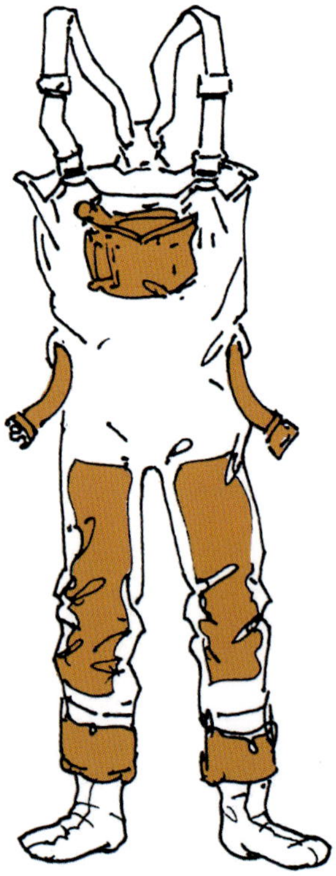

Stocking-Foot Chest Waders

Look for waders with attached wading belt, front pocket, reinforced knees, and gravel guards. A good pair will cost from $150 and up. Carry a patch kit if you're traveling.

3

Fly-Fishing Gear

Fly-fishing can be gear intensive. The basic components of rod, reel, line, leader and tippet will get you started fishing on almost any trout river. But other factors, including our own safety on or in the water, mean we often need considerably more equipment and tools. The following items will help you understand which equipment you need and their uses on the river; feel free to adapt these lists to your specific needs.

I use two bags for all my equipment. One is a large duffel to carry my larger gear such as waders, wading boots, vest, jacket, insulating garments, wading staff, and net. I like bags which have a separate compartment for carrying wet gear after I get off the river. My second bag is smaller and has compartments for carrying extra reels and spools, fly boxes, leaders, tippet spools, camera, insect repellent, sunscreen, etc. Waterproof bags are especially nice for boats.

Chest Waders

More often than not, you will want to get in the river to fish. In summer, when water is low, this may not be a problem; but when the water is cold and deep, or you have to walk through a lot of brush or marshy areas to get to the river, it's a good idea to have a pair of waders.

Modern chest waders come in three types: rubber, neoprene and Gore-Tex. Rubber waders should be avoided because they are dangerous and uncomfortable. Gore-Tex is the material of choice for most anglers because it is lightweight, breathable, and will last for years. You will pay more for Gore-Tex, but the benefits are worth the price. Gore-Tex waders are not insulated, however, so it will be necessary to wear warm underclothes.

Neoprene waders are similar to wetsuit material, come in various weights or thicknesses, and are insulated; they work well in extremely cold conditions. Neoprene waders also cost less and are a good compromise for anglers on a budget.

Waders can be purchased with attached boots or bootless (stocking-foot). For fit, comfort and versatility, it is recommended that you consider bootless waders and purchase a separate pair of boots that give you a comfortable fit and good ankle support comparable to a good hiking boot. Always wear socks with stocking-foot waders.

In addition to chest waders, one can buy hip-boot waders and waist-high waders. Unless you absolutely know you will not be in water past your knees, chest waders will be your most versatile option.

Wading Boots

The most important elements when considering a wading boot are comfort, weight, ankle support, and the type of sole. Comfort, weight and ankle support are different from boot to boot, so it pays to try on several brands prior to making your purchase. Choose a boot by trying them on with your waders. Most companies have a range of boots to fit a range of budgets. More expensive boots are made from leather and can be heavy or lightweight. The trend is towards lightweight boots, which have their obvious benefits. Wading sandals are also available, but have limited application because they offer very little ankle support and easily fill with debris such as sand and small rocks.

The type of sole you choose depends on the rivers you fish. There are three types to choose from: felted, studded, and rubber. Felted is a good all-around sole. It offers excellent traction when you're scrambling over boulders and moss-covered rocks, and it's better for wearing in boats. Cleated soles are better for slippery conditions such as mossy rocks, but offer slightly less traction because less of the sole comes in contact with the ground. Rubber soles are another good option when slippery conditions are not a problem. Some boots now come with the option of sole inserts so you can choose the sole that best fits the conditions of the day. Inserts are a great idea, but with the obvious weak point concerning the connection points.

Wading Boots

Used in conjunction with stocking-foot waders. May have cleats or other traction devices.

Jacket

Hooded waterproof or windproof wading jackets are short so they do not hang in the water and come with large breast pockets to hold lots of gear. Velcro cuffs are nice to keep water out of your sleeve when needing to reach down into the water.

Wading Jacket

Wading jackets are rain jackets designed for anglers to wear over the top of their waders. These are a better alternative to standard rain jackets because they are extra short and will not drag in the water. Wading jackets also come with oversized pockets to hold tackle and tool attachments, thus they can function as a vest. I recommend jackets that come with waterproof cuffs to help keep out water. When I wear my wading jacket I use the jacket as my vest and wear a lanyard around my neck to hold my tools and tippet.

Wading Staff

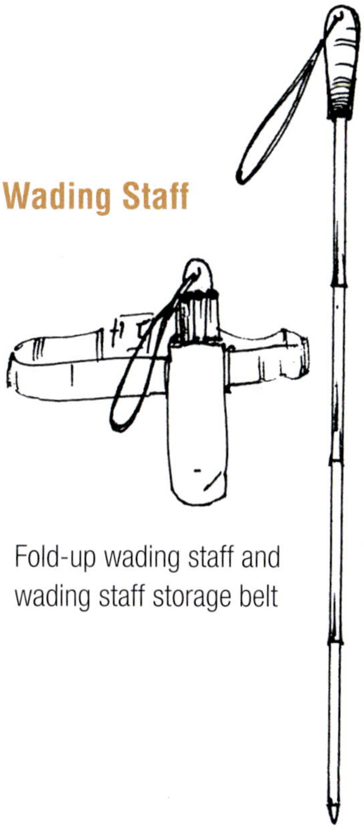

Fold-up wading staff and wading staff storage belt

Wading Staff

Wading staffs can be handy, especially when you're moving over slippery rocks or contending with current or varying river depths. There are one-piece and breakdown models. Breakdown models are easier to carry around and can be carried in a holster on your hip when not in use.

Vest or Pack

Vests, a mainstay of fly-anglers for years, have been re-conceptualized over recent years to include a variety of choices such as waist packs,

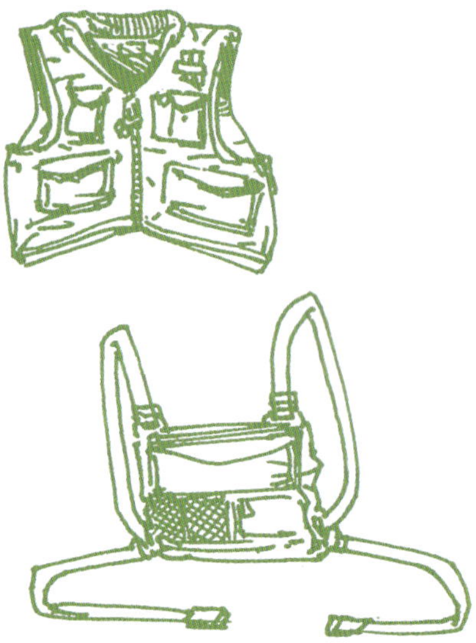

Traditional Fishing Vest and Chest Pack

Both are good options and appeal to different approaches to fishing. A vest will hold more gear and can be better for extended hikes; chest packs hold a minimum of gear for the minimalist and short walks that may not require extra gear or food.

harness packs, chest packs and hybrid vests with backpacks. All have their pros and cons, as do the traditional style vests, and some of them are geared towards specific styles of fishing. The vest or pack you choose should have the capacity to carry all your tackle and fly boxes, have convenient pockets and be comfortable. I recommend beginning with a traditional style vest because they have proven themselves as the best option.

Net

A small portable net is a great idea, if for no other reason than it makes life easier for the fish. Handling and landing a fish without a net is hard on the fish because it takes more time and you invariably have to handle the fish with your hands, which isn't good for the fish. Purchase a net which can be carried on the back of your pack or vest for convenience. The recommended "no kill nets" which have rubber or rubber-coated netting are the best option for the safety of the fish; they are also less frustrating for the angler because hooks rarely get tangled in them.

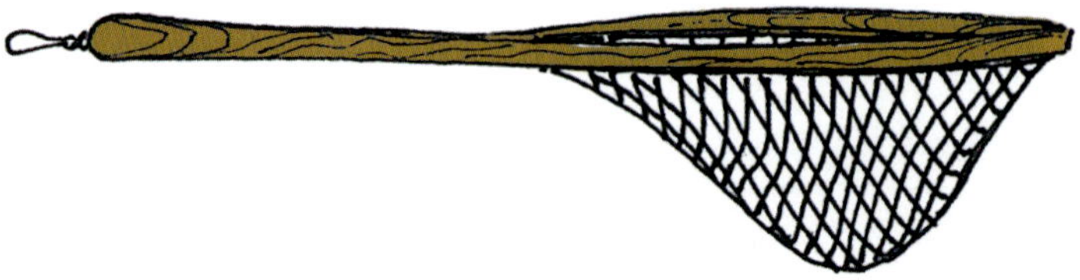

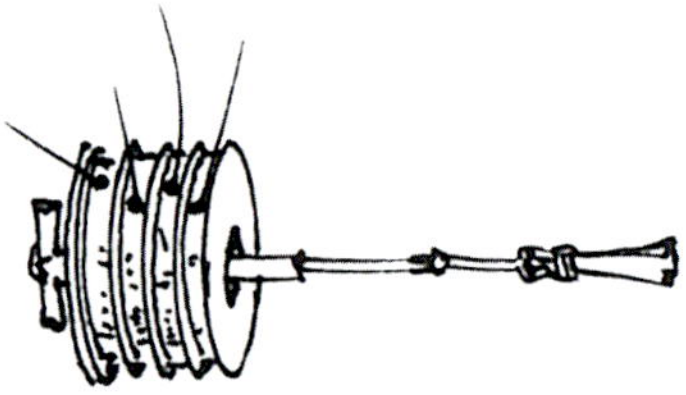

Tippet Spool Carrier

Fly Boxes

Fly boxes are important because they help with organization and protect your flies from getting lost or damaged. Anglers may carry a box for each type of fly, such as streamers, dry flies, and nymphs. Some boxes have extra compartments for strike indicators and split shot. Waterproof boxes are a good idea and will prevent flies from getting wet and rusting in your box. Start with one box for all your flies and expand as you acquire more flies.

Tippet Spool Carriers

Carry several tippet spools that can be clipped to your vest or lanyard for easy access.

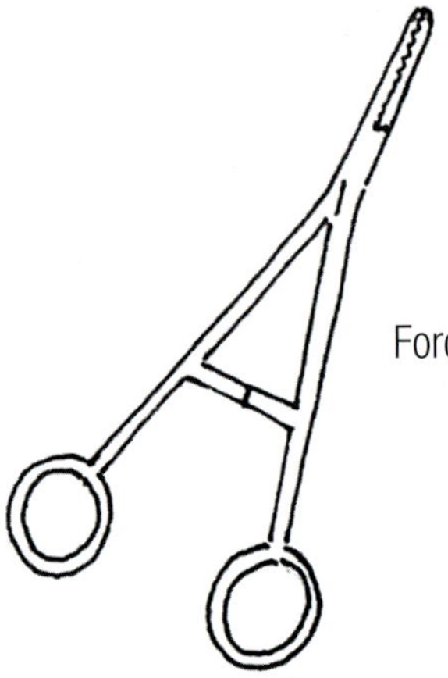

Forceps

Forceps

Forceps are used for removing hooks from fish, pinching hook barbs, and securing split shot onto leaders. Some forceps come with scissors and hook-eye cleaners, both of which are nice features.

Knot-Tying Tool

As the name implies, this is used for tying a variety of knots, especially nail knots. I use a Tie-Fast knot tier for tying all my nail knots.

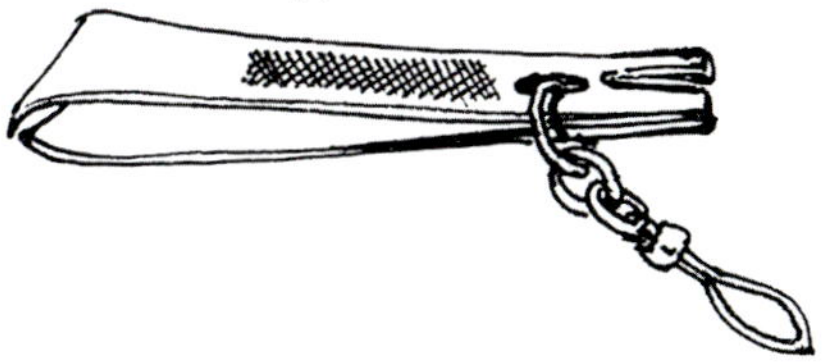
Nippers

Hook Threader

This is a small looped wire used to draw tippet through the eye of the hook. Simply push the small wire through the eye of the hook, thread the tag end of the leader through the wire loop, and pull back through the eye. Your hook will be threaded and you're ready to tie your knot. People with fading eyesight or unsteady hands will particularly want one of these. Anyone can appreciate them in low-light conditions. Some fly boxes come with hook threaders.

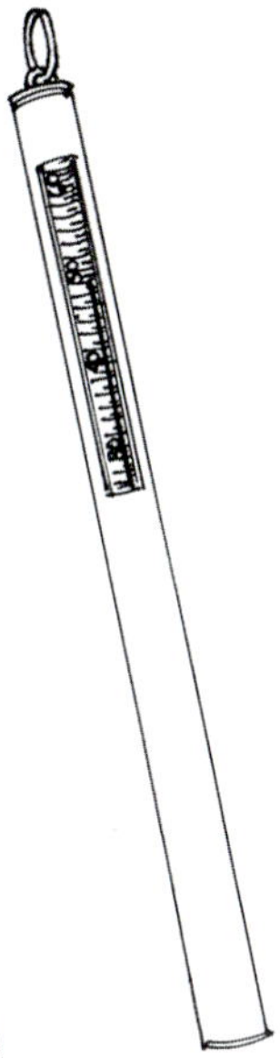
Thermometer

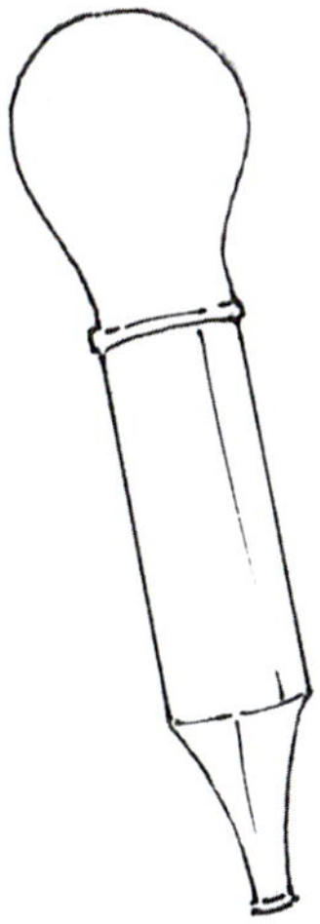
Stomach Pump

Nippers

Nippers, which are used for clipping line, leader, tippet and the tag ends of knots, are a much better option than using your teeth—just ask your dentist. Choose nippers that are sharp, angled at 45 degrees and come with a small needle for cleaning out the eyes of flies. If you fish a lot, nippers will have to be replaced frequently because they get dull or lose their spring. Expensive nippers are worth the money, but because they go dull and can't be re-sharpened I avoid ones with multi-functions such as a knot-tying tool. Nail clippers are an alternative to nippers, but I find they lack sharpness and a fine cutting area needed for close trimming.

Thermometer

This is not necessary, but it can offer some clues to what the fish may be doing in relation to water temperature.

Polypropylene

Foam

Plastic Bubble

Stomach Pump

This is for the fish, not you! Pumps are used for sampling the content of the stomachs of trout. There are right and wrong ways to use a stomach pump, so read the directions that come with it. Some anglers claim this is too invasive to the fish, but biologists will tell you it does no harm.

Strike Indicators

Used for nymphing, indicators come in a variety of forms, such as foam balls, bunched polypropylene, sticky foam, putty, and plastic tubes.

Strike indicators should float under the weight of your nymphs, be easy to apply and remove from your line, and not hinder casting.

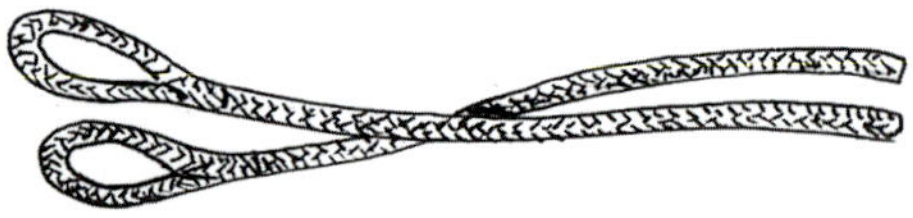

Braided Loop Connectors

One option to connect fly line to leaders. (See also loop-to-loop connectors.)

Braided Loop Connectors

These connectors allow you to add a loop onto the end of your fly line for loop system connectors. I always carry an extra packet to replace frayed or worn-out connectors.

Dry-Fly Floatant

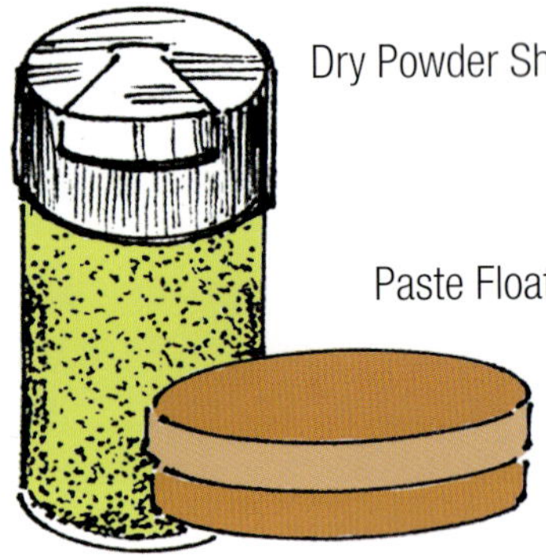

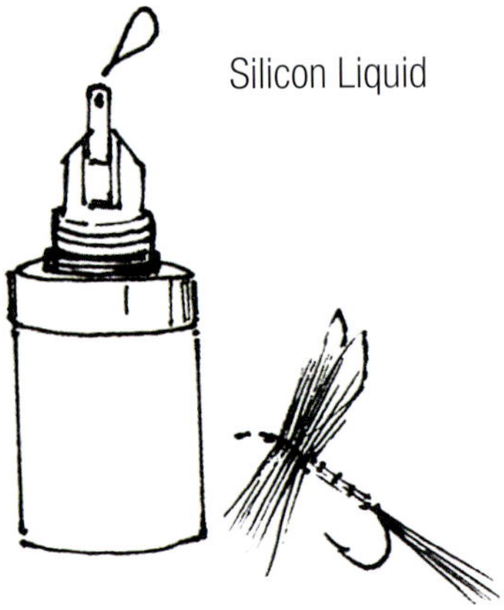

Weight

Weights attach to your leader and are generally small to enable proper casting. They come in a variety of forms: split shot, putty, lead strips, and non-toxic or lead-free. Check local regulations, because some states ban the use of lead weight or any kind of external weight on your line.

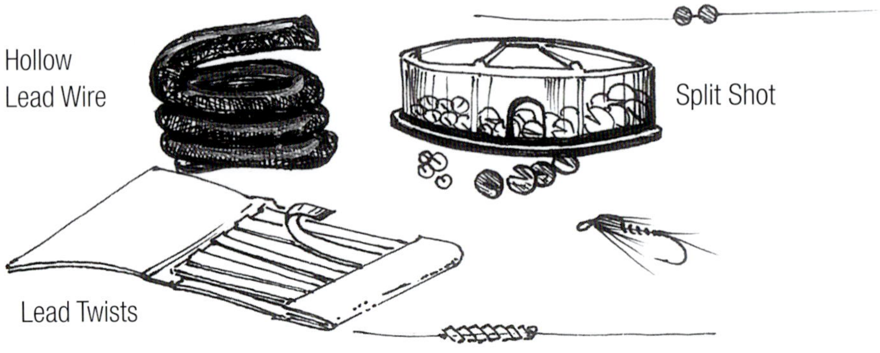

Floatant

Imperative for dry-fly fishing, floatant usually comes in a gel or paste and is applied to the fly to keep it buoyant. Also consider a drying agent such as powder or a dry-fly patch for absorbing the water out of waterlogged flies.

Dry-Fly Crystals

This powder can be added to a dry fly or wet fly to create the effect of tiny air bubbles, thereby giving a more realistic look to your flies.

Lanyard

This is a necklace with tool attachments for carrying tippet spools, nippers, floatant, and other small items. They can be useful if you do not wear a vest or fish from a boat.

Clothing

Cold weather insulated clothing that can be worn under Gore-Tex waders. Lightweight sun clothing.

Safety Accessories

First-aid kit, sunscreen, insect repellent, sun hat, wool cap, fingerless gloves, wader-repair kit, utility knife.

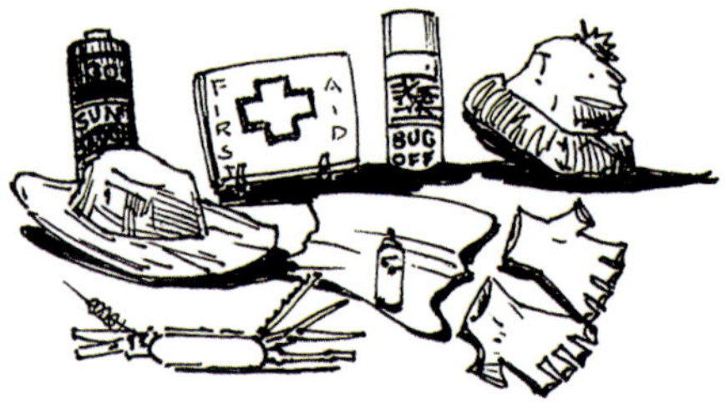

Polarizing Sunglasses

Do not leave home without them. Critical for eye protection against harmful sun rays and fish hooks. They are also a great fish-spotting tool because they cut the surface glare of the water. Avoid cheap sunglasses which have poor optics and can put strain on your eyes. For the best optics, purchase high-quality glass lenses with an amber tint and photochromatic coating. Avoid mirror-coated lenses which can cast glare onto the water. Polycarbonate lenses are a cheaper alternative and weigh less than glass, but are optically inferior.

Binoculars

An underrated piece of fly-fishing equipment, binoculars are useful for spotting rising fish up and down stream.

Camera

For catch-and-release anglers, this may be your only consolation to not mounting that big trophy trout. Consider buying a waterproof housing or case for your camera.

Clothing

For summer fishing I choose quick-drying clothing which is also rated for sun protection. I also use ventilated long-sleeve shirts and zip-off nylon pants. In colder weather, I also go with synthetics that are quick drying, moisture wicking, and insulated. At no time do I use any cotton clothing, because when it's wet, even on a sunny hot day, it can expose you to the elements and create hypothermia.

I always choose clothing which can help camouflage my presence by matching the backdrop of my surroundings. I buy clothing in earth-tone colors such as browns and greens, and stay away from bright colors such as reds, oranges, and yellows.

Here are a few other items I carry on my person or in my gear bag: first-aid kit, compact scissors, bug spray and head netting, wide-brim sun hat, stocking cap, fingerless gloves, eyeglass cleaning cloth and solution, sunscreen, multi-tool with knife, pliers and small screwdriver.

4

Knots & Rigging Connections

Every experienced angler knows that knots are an important part of fishing; they are the vital connection points in our tackle, and they can make the difference between catching and not catching fish. Know your knots and develop good knot-tying habits! Once you have learned the knots, practice them before you go fishing, and do so in the wind, heat, cold and rain. This will give you some idea of the potential conditions you will face on a river— along with the excitement of rising fish, of course.

In this chapter you are going to learn the knots and rigging connections for a basic fly-fishing set-up. The rigging connections are: fly-line backing to reel, fly-line backing to fly line, fly line to leader, leader to tippet, and tippet to fly (see illustration below). Different knots are used for each connection and all serve a specific purpose related to strength, bulk, and performance.

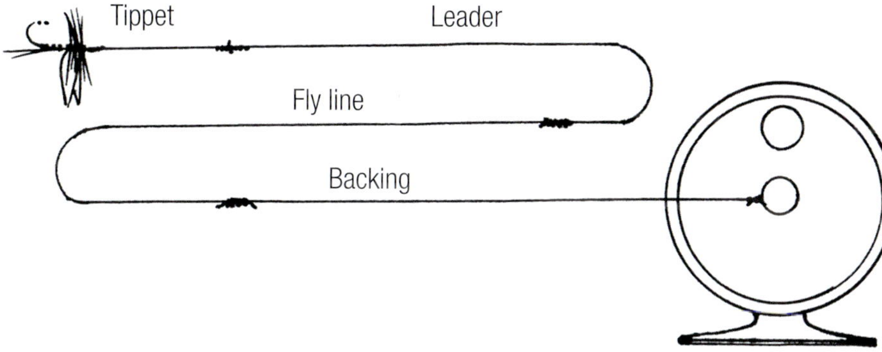

Basic Connections

Fly-line backing to reel, backing to fly line, fly line to tapered leader, tapered leader to tippet, tippet to fly.

Knots are for both function and performance. Functionally, our knots should have a high breaking strength, and not all knots do. A simple overhand knot is almost never used in fishing's most terminal connections because it is weak when put under pressure. Strong knots can only be tied if we use reliable materials and develop good knot-tying habits. If you need to budget your expenses, do so with rods, reels and other gear, but buy the best possible line, leader and tippet money can buy.

The condition of your line is an important part of a knots effectiveness. Never tie knots on line that has been frayed or nicked with use. Discard monofilament that is more than one year old because it's prone to breakdown by exposure to sunlight.

The act of tightening, or seating, a knot is also critical. You will improve the strength of any knot and help it seat properly by moistening it with saliva or water prior to drawing it tight. When tightening a knot, do so slowly and evenly to ensure proper seating

Rigging Connections & Recommended Knots

- Backing to Spool: Arbor Knot
- Backing to Fly Line: Albright or Nail Knot
- Fly Line to Leader: Nail Knot or Loop System with Perfection Loop or Braided Loop Connectors
- Leader to Tippet: Blood or Surgeon's Knot
- Tippet to Fly: Clinch, Improved Clinch, Trilene, Orvis Loop, Duncan Loop

Knots are the vital connection points in our tackle, and they can make the difference between catching and not catching fish.

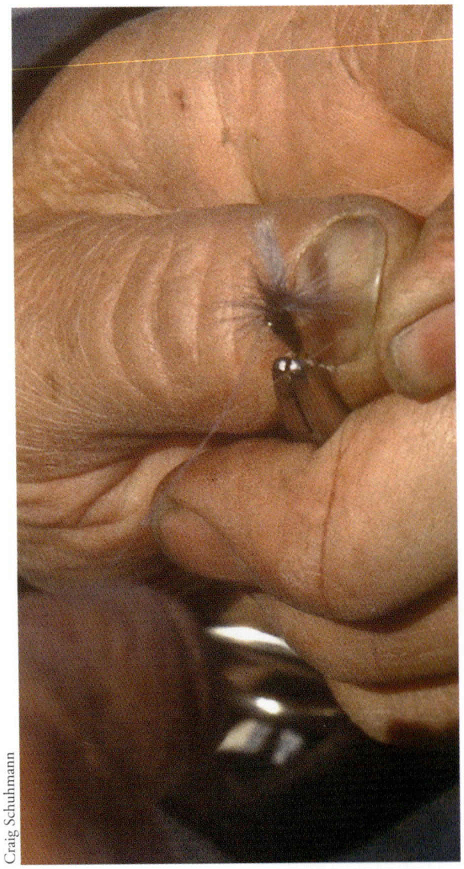

Dick Winter tying a Black Drake.

and reduce friction. Pay attention to which ends of the line need to be pulled to cinch the knot; some knots require more than two ends to be pulled. As the knot comes together, increase tension and test the knot with the strength in your hands and arms. If it is a poorly tied knot it will only break when under tension.

Be sure to trim the tag ends of a knot carefully with a sharp pair of nippers or scissors, as close to the knot as possible, cutting at a 45-degree angle. Finally, always inspect the knot visually. A well-tied knot should look neat and have well-seated wraps. Take the time to retie any knot you don't trust.

Knots perform to make our equipment run smoothly, but they can also affect the way trout react to our presentation. Bulky or poorly trimmed knots will catch in the fly-rod guides, snag line when spooled onto the reel, or pick up debris in the water. All these effects can result in casting difficulty, lost fish, spooked fish or broken gear. For the same reasons, knots should also facilitate a straight-line connection between two materials, rather than an angled connection. Some knots, such as those that connect a fly, can affect the way trout perceive our fly in the water.

In the directions below, "tag end" refers to working the fly end of the line. "Standing line" refers to the portion of line leading to the rod or reel.

Backing to Reel

Fly-line backing is secured to the spool arbor of the reel with an arbor knot (aka, reel knot). This is a simple but strong knot which in most cases will never be tested because it is buried so far in the reel.

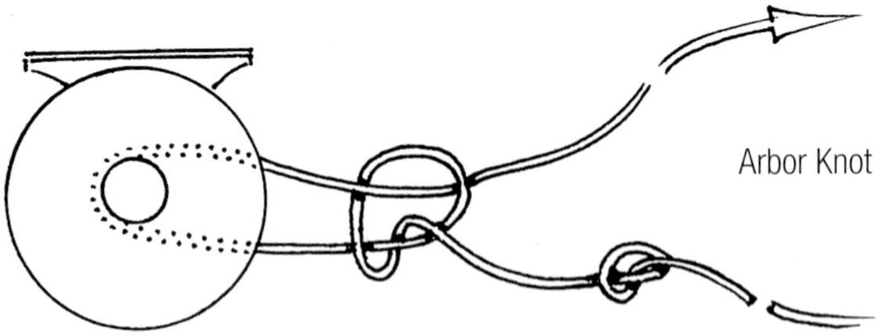

Tying the Arbor Knot

With the spool on the reel, thread the running end of the backing through the line guide on the reel housing and around the spool so that it meets up with the standing line of the backing. With the tag end of the backing, tie an overhand knot around the standing part of the backing. Tie another overhand knot at the end of the tag end. Pull on the standing part of the backing, snugging together the two knots so they are tight against the spool surface. Trim the tag end.

Wind on the proper amount of backing so it feeds off at the bottom of the reel. If your line is feeding off the top of the reel you have wound the backing in the wrong direction.

Backing to Fly Line

Fly line is attached to your backing with a nail knot or an Albright knot. Both of these knots are small, have a high breaking strength, and create a straight connection between fly line and backing. If you are using a weight-forward line, be sure to attach the butt end of the line to your backing. The butt end is usually labeled on new fly lines. If you're unsure because it's not labeled, then look for the end of the fly line that's thickest in the first 30 feet. The thick end is the front of your fly line.

Albright Knot

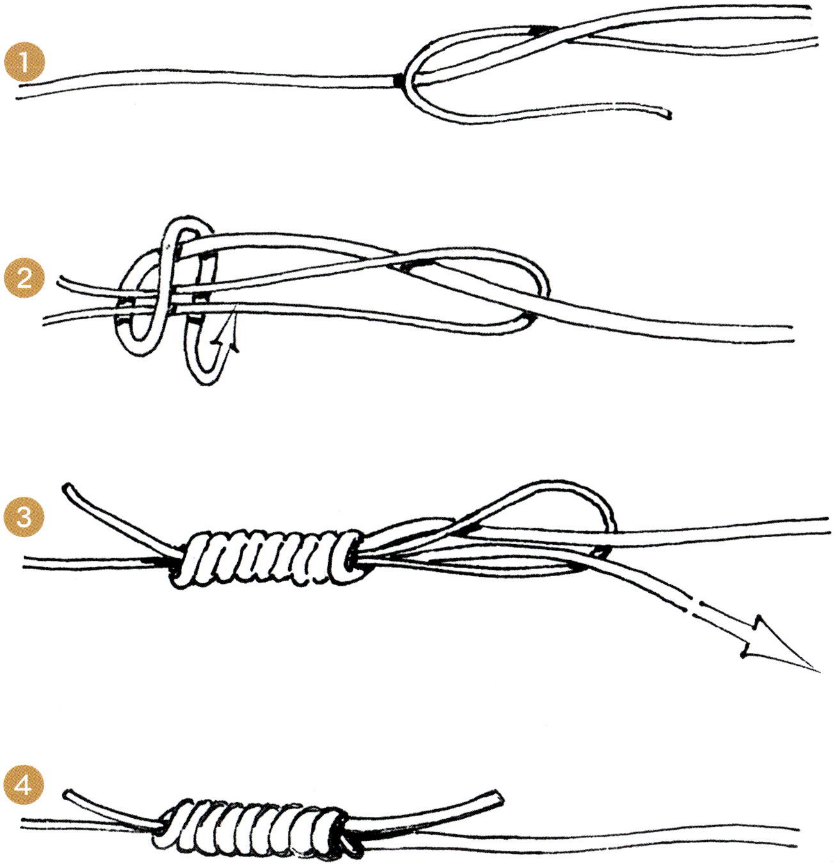

Tying the Albright Knot

1 Double back the tag end of the fly line to form a four-inch loop.

2 Holding the loop in one hand, feed the tag end of the backing through one side of the loop in the fly line. Extend the backing about 10 inches beyond the loop.

3 Pinch the backing in the same hand holding the loop and begin wrapping the tag end of the backing in tight wraps, over both strands of fly line and backing, moving towards the loop end of the fly line. Make 10 to 12 wraps and push the tag end of the backing through the looped fly line on the same side it entered the loop so both standing and tag end of the backing are aligned together. Pull on the standing part of the backing to tighten the wraps and then pull on both ends of the backing, sliding the wraps towards the end of the looped fly line.

4 Keep working the wraps toward the end of the loop until you reach the end of the loop, but don't go beyond it. Moisten the knot and pull hard on the tag and standing end of the fly line and backing. Clip off the tag ends of both the fly line and backing close to the knot.

Tying the Nail Knot

1 Align the tube end of the fly line, allowing about 3 inches of the tag end of the fly line to stick out beyond the tube.

2 Holding the tube and fly line in one hand, form a loop in the butt-end of your backing, leaving a tag of three to four inches. Align backing, fly line and tube, with the looped end of the backing facing your hand. Pinching together fly line, tube and backing in one hand, wrap the tag end of the backing in tight wraps away from your hand. Pass the tag end of the leader through the tube. Slide out the tube from under the wraps, pinching the wraps together so they do not separate.

3 Still pinching the wraps, pull gently on both ends of the leader to tighten the wraps in place. Let go of wraps and pull on both ends of the leader until the wraps are tightly snug against the fly line. Wraps should be smooth and aligned side-by-side rather than bunched-up together. Pull tightly on the leader and fly line to test the knot. Clip both tag ends of the fly line and leader.

Nail Knot

Nail knots require some type of tool, originally a nail, but more effectively a small-diameter hollow tube. There are several good nail-knot tying tools on the market, such as Tie -Fast, and I recommend purchasing one and keeping it attached to your vest. The following are instructions for tying with a hollow tube.

1

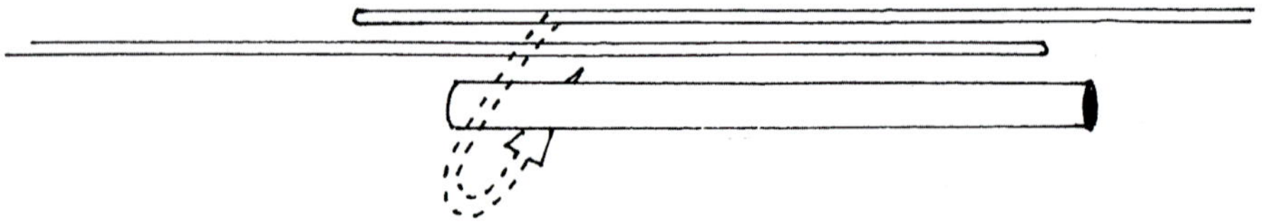

2

3

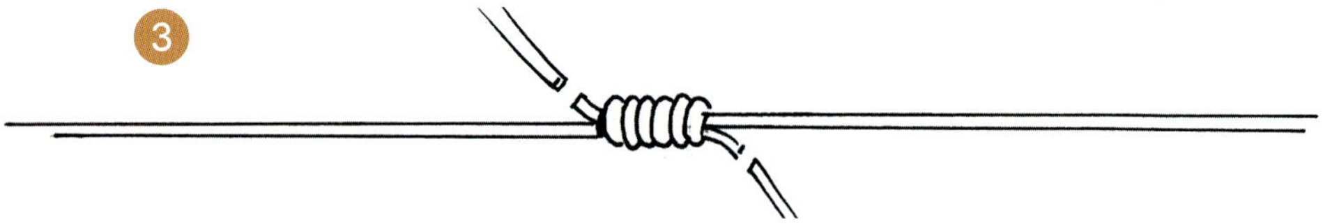

Good knots are critical and allow our equipment to operate smoothly and correctly.

Fly Line to Leader

The best knot for connecting your fly line to your leader is the nail knot in the diagram on page 36, but many fly line and leader manufacturers have gone to a loop-connection system for an easier, faster connection. These are pre-tied loops in the tip of the fly line and butt-end of the leader. The two loops are then joined together. If there are no pre-tied loops you can add them to your fly line with a braided loop connector, then tie a perfection loop in the butt-end of your leader to attach the two. Alternatively, you can nail knot an 8 inch piece of 15-20 pound test to the end of your fly line and tie a perfection loop at the tag end. This perfection loop can then be attached to the perfection loop at the end of your tapered leader. The diagrams below show you the proper way to connect two loops. On page 34 you'll find how to tie a perfection loop.

There is a right method and a wrong method for joining two loops. The right method is to thread the loop of the fly line through the loop of the leader and then feed the tag end of the leader through the bottom side of the fly-line loop. This will form a straight connection without pinching the loop. To disconnect the loops simply reverse the pressure by pushing the loops together. The wrong method involves threading the leader loop through the fly-line loop and passing the tip of the leader through the loop in the leader. This makes for a weaker connection that is hard to separate.

The best knot for connecting your fly line to your leader is the nail knot.

There is a right method and a wrong method for joining two loops.

Correct Loop-to-Loop Connection

Loops Slide Together

Incorrect Loop-to-Loop Connection

One Loop is Bent Over Another

Craig Schuhmann

Tying the Perfection Loop

Perfection loops create a straight connection between the loop and the leader.

1 Form a loop with the tag end of the leader on the back side of the standing section of line. Tag end should be off to the right. Allow three to four inches of tag past the standing portion of line.

2 Form a smaller loop in front of the first, holding it in place between your thumb and forefinger.

3 Pass the tag end of the leader in-between the first and second loop and hold it in place.

4 Pull the second loop through the first loop, being sure not to let go of the tag end of leader.

5 Pull tight on the second loop to cinch the knot. Tag end should come off the cinched knot at a right angle.

6 Clip the tag end. Loop size can be adjusted by making either a smaller or larger second loop.

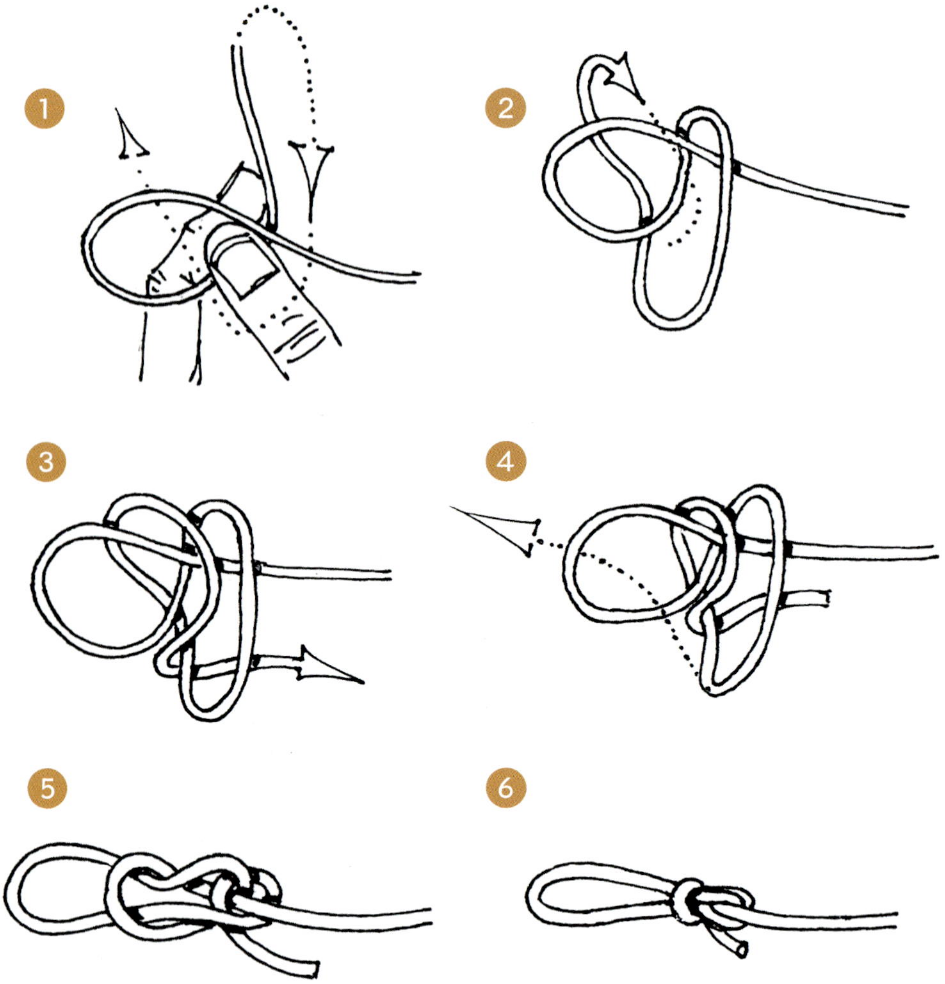

A display of "double grins".

Leader to Tippet

The surgeon's knot and blood knot (aka, barrel knot) are both used to connect tippet to the end of leader. More people use a surgeon's knot than a blood knot because it's easier, but the surgeon's knot is weaker, has more bulk, and creates a slight angle between the leader and tippet. I would encourage you to learn the blood knot, which is nothing more than a two-sided clinch knot.

Surgeon's Knot (weaker)

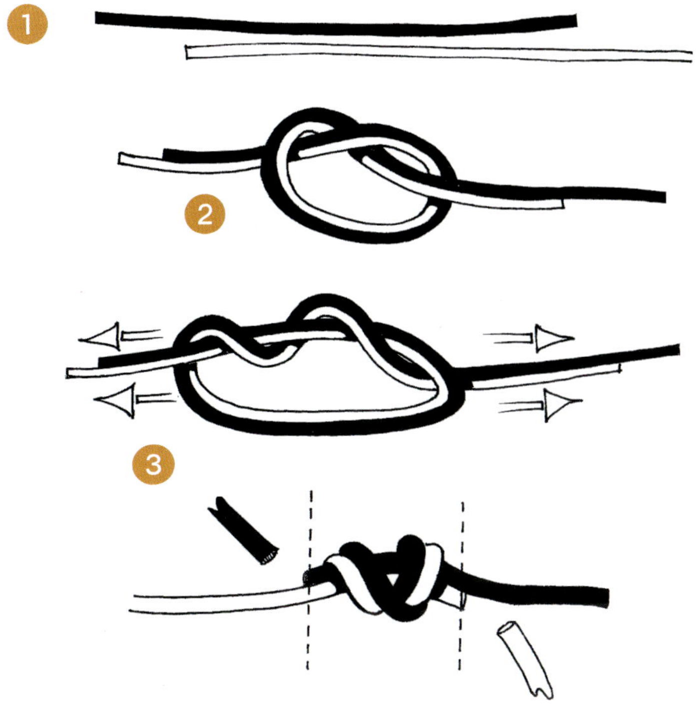

Blood Knot (stronger)

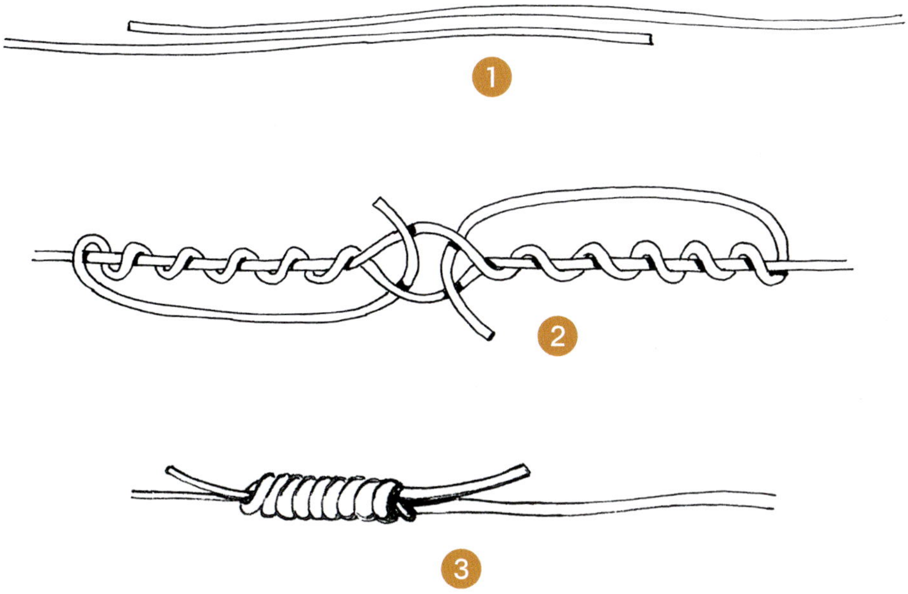

Tying the Surgeon's Knot

1. Align the tag ends of two pieces of monofilament opposite each other.

2. Form a loop with the doubled-over line and create an overhand knot by bringing the tag end of the leader and the entire standing line of the tippet through the loop.

3. Form a second overhand loop. Tighten the knot by pulling both the standing lines and tag ends in opposite directions. Clip the tag ends.

Tying the Blood Knot

Blood knots are strong, produce small knots that slide easily through guides, and create a straight connection between tippet and leader. Blood knots require some practice to perfect.

1. Start by crossing the tag end of the leader and butt end of the tippet and holding them together with your thumb and forefinger.

2. Wrap the tag end of the tippet five or six times around the standing line of the leader and thread through the gap where your fingers are holding the crossed lines.

3. Do the same with the other side, wrapping the tag end of the leader five or six times around the standing line of the tippet and thread through the same gap where the lines cross, but in the opposite direction.

4. Tighten by pulling both the tag ends of each and the standing lines in the opposite directions.

Tippet to Fly

Several knots can be used to attach a fly to the end of your leader, and they come in two forms, a cinched knot and a loop. The cinch knots place the knot down to the eye of the hook. Cinch knots are stiff connections good for attaching dry flies. Loop knots create a loop in front of the hook eye allowing the fly to move freely on the tippet. Loop knots are good for nymphs, streamers and wet flies. Cinch knots include the clinch knot, improved clinch, and Trilene knot. Loop knots include the Duncan loop and Orvis loop.

Tying the Clinch Knot

1. Pass the tag end of the tippet through the eye of the hook, forming a loop just above the eye of the hook.
2. Make five to seven turns with the tag end of the tippet around the standing line of the tippet. Thread the tag end through the loop near the eye of the hook.
3. Tighten by pulling the running line tight.
4. To create an improved clinch knot: after threading the tag end through the loop near the hook eye, pass it through the loop created when you threaded the tag end through the loop near the eye of the hook.

Clinch Knot

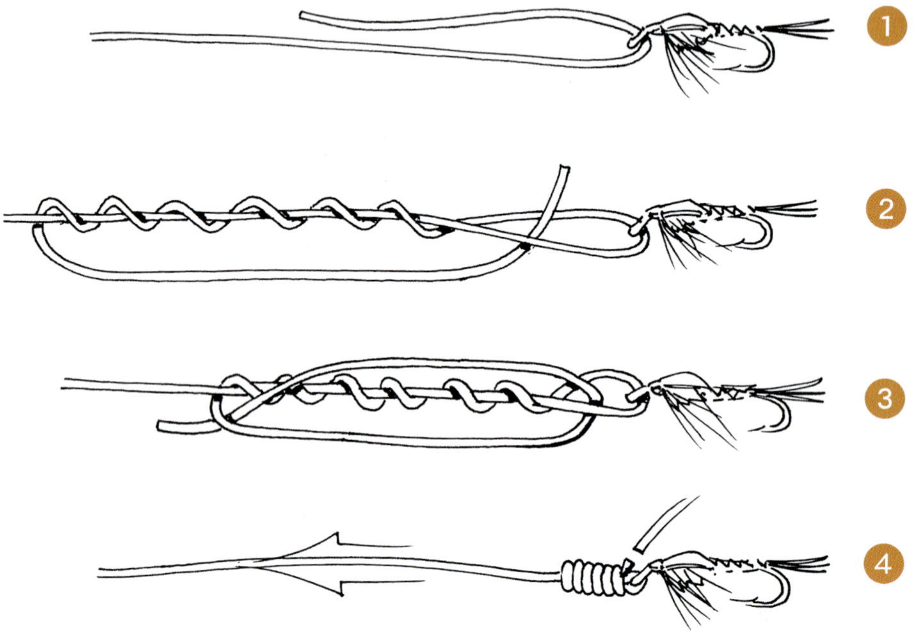

Tying the Trilene Knot

Follow the instructions for the clinch knot but rather than threading the tag end of the tippet through the eye once, thread it twice. Be sure to take the tag end through both loops near the hook eye prior to cinching the knot.

Trilene Knot

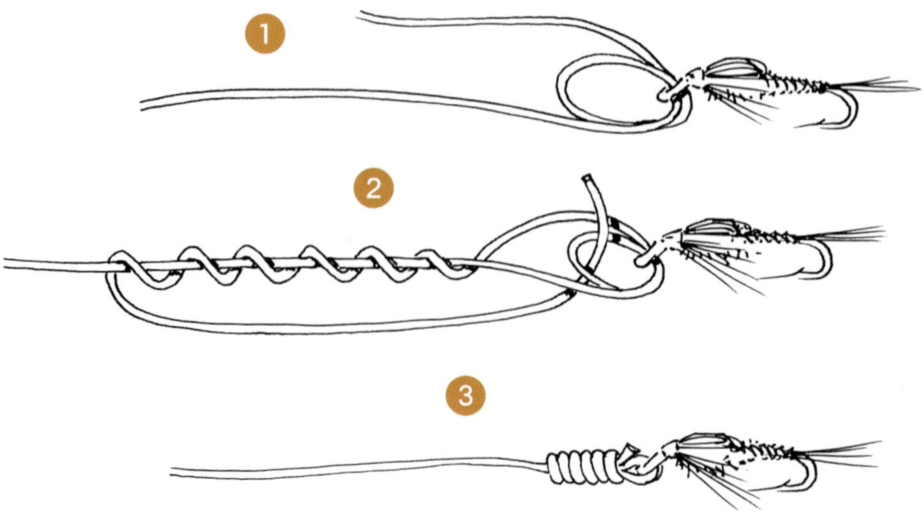

Duncan Loop and Orvis Loop

Both these loops are useful when you want the fly to move freely on the tippet.

Duncan Loop

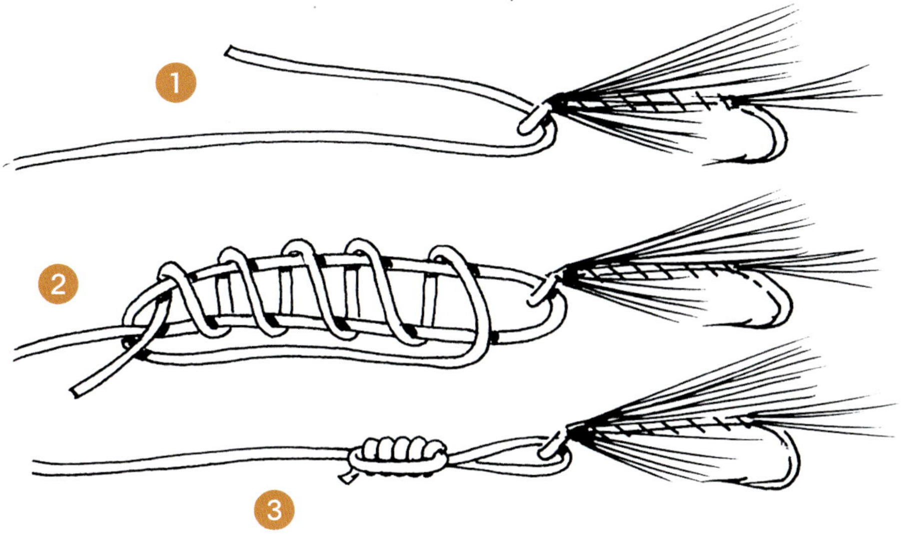

Tying the Duncan Loop

1 Create a loop by threading the eye of the hook with the tag end of the tippet extending 6-8 inches. Form another small loop with the tag end.

2 Make five or six turns with the tag end around the first loop moving away from the fly.

3 Moisten and tighten the knot by pulling the tag end. How tight you cinch the knot will determine whether it can be slid up or down on the leader for an open or closed loop. Adjust the loop and trim tag end.

Orvis Loop

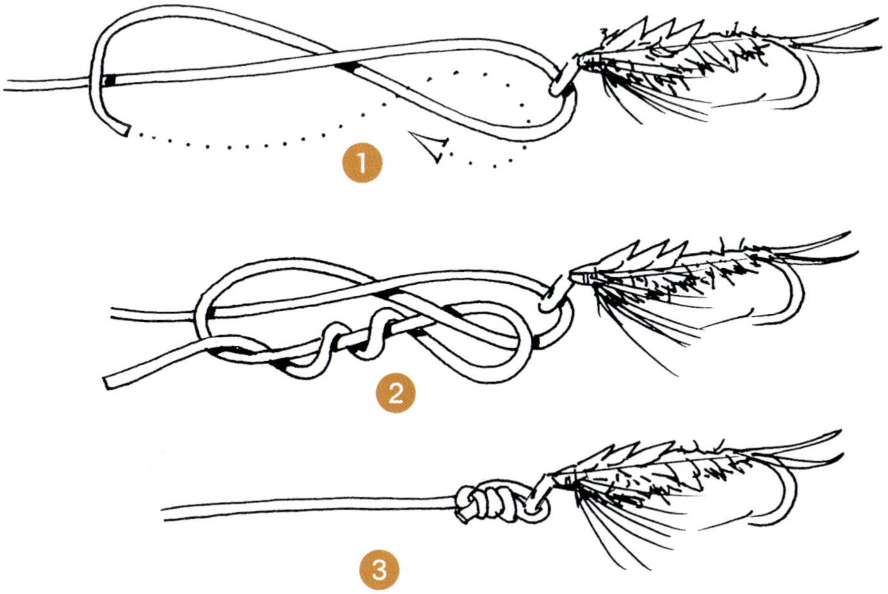

Tying the Orvis Loop

1 Form a loop by threading the tag end of the tippet through the eye of the hook, allowing for 6-8 inches of tag.

2 Form a second loop by bringing the tag around the standing line and back through the first loop. Thread the tag back through the second loop and make two turns around the side of the loop.

3 Moisten and tighten the knot against the standing line to form the loop and trim the tag ends.

5

Casting

Fly-fishing relies on the weight of the fly line, not the fly or external weight, which is released incrementally with each casting stroke until a desired distance is reached.

"It is not easy to tell one how to cast. The art must be acquired by practice."
~Charles Orvis-1883~

If we examine that which separates fly-fishing from all other forms of fishing, we would have to begin with the cast. All other methods of fishing rely on a weighted lure or external weight to carry the fishing line off the reel. A spin-angler can throw his lure or bait rig long distances with one casting stroke. Fly-fishing, on the other hand, attempts to cast a fly, a speck of material which weighs nothing, long distances. Fly-fishing relies on the weight of the fly line, not the fly or external weight, which is released incrementally with each casting stroke until a desired distance is reached. Referred to as the false cast, this is the back-and-forth motion one sees during a fly-cast. The mechanics of good casting are achieved with a proper stroke which allows for an efficient transfer of energy between the rod and fly line; in other words, no slack. This transfer of energy allows the line to move in a controlled path above the water.

Craig Schuhmann

In this chapter, we will cover a few basic principles that will help you understand how to cast correctly. We will then learn some different casts and note their appropriate uses. Lastly, we will identify a few casting problems and ways to fix them. The skills you will learn in this chapter will form the foundation for understanding and implementing the techniques discussed in the chapter on presentation.

Fly-casting is not difficult when accuracy and presentation do not matter, and most people can learn to cast 30 feet or more in less than an hour with no instruction. If you do not believe me, try it! Before reading any further, grab your fly rod, find a lawn, set up a target about 40 feet from your casting position and try to hit the target. I will wait . . .

How did you do? Were you able to hit the target eventually? Did the line straighten out in front of you or did it bunch-up in piles once it hit the ground? Did you hit yourself with the line? Learning to fly-cast is about learning to correct mistakes. The more you cast, the more you will develop a feel for achieving the goals of distance and accuracy, and many casting problems will fix themselves.

There are three basic parts to a cast: the stroke, arch, and loop. Study these definitions in relation to the diagrams.

Most people can learn to cast 30 feet or more in less than an hour with no instruction. If you do not believe me, try it!

There are three basic parts to a cast: the stroke, arch, and loop. Study these definitions in relation to the diagrams.

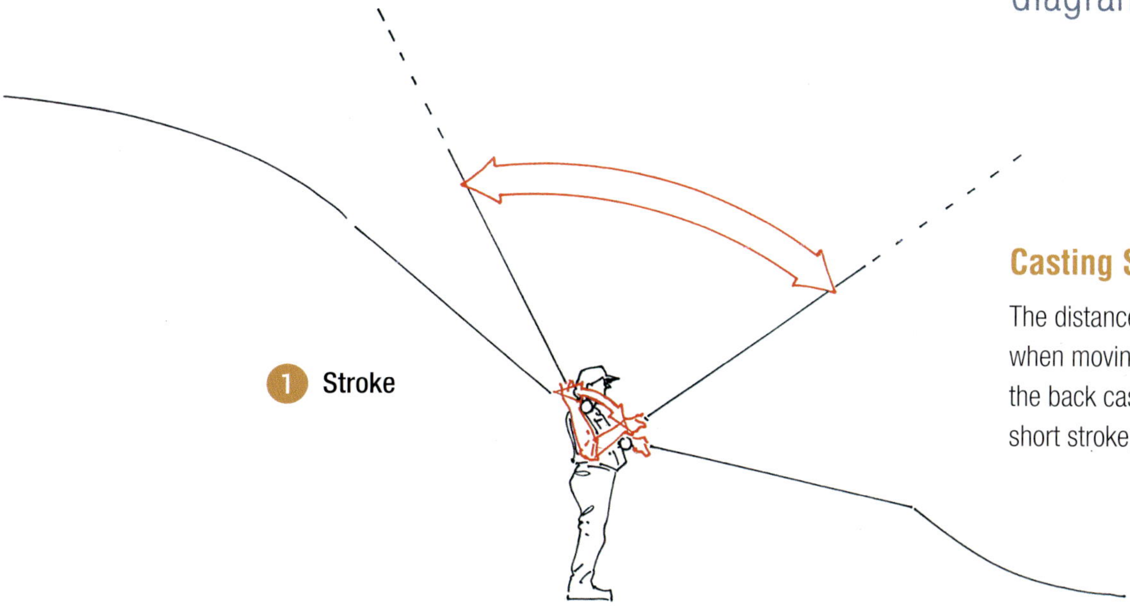

Casting Stroke

The distance your rod hand travels when moving from the forward cast to the back cast or vica versa. Short cast, short stroke; long cast, long stroke.

Casting stroke refers to the entire movement of the rod from the starting to stopping position. This is the distance your rod hand travels when moving from the forward cast to the back cast or vice versa. The stroke, combined with the weight of the fly line, applies power or bend to the rod, which in turns propels the fly line in a straight-line path. This process is known as "loading and unloading the rod".

Proper loading and unloading of the rod can only occur with the proper application of power during the stroke. A proper stroke begins with a steady pull of the rod from the starting position and ends with a sudden acceleration and abrupt stop, or in the words of casting guru Mel Krieger, "a whump." The easiest way to conceive of this movement is to think about what it would take to throw a tomato off the end of a stick so that it flies straight out in front of you.

Casting Arch showing Stopping Points on Forward and Back Cast

Stopping the rod at the 10:00 position on the back cast and 2:00 position on the forward cast are good starting points for achieving the proper casting arch. A short cast will have a narrow casting arch; a longer cast, a wider casting arch.

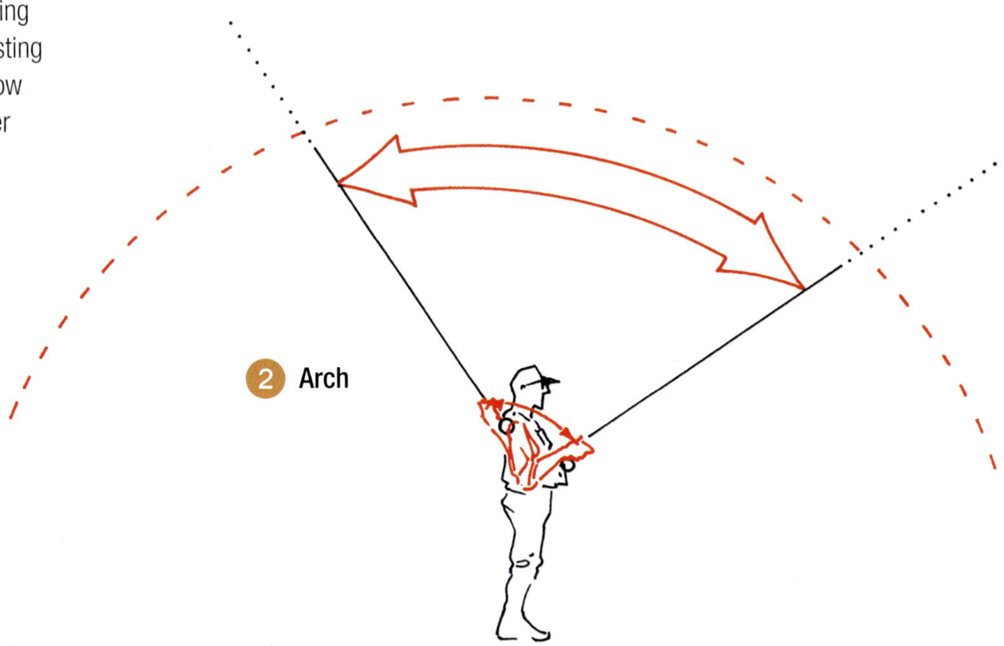

Proper loading and unloading of the rod can only occur with the proper application of power during the stroke.

Short strokes which require minimal power have narrow arcs, and long strokes, which require more power, have wider arcs.

How much power is applied during the cast depends on how far you are casting and the amount of line extending out of the rod tip. Short casts, under 30 feet, require a short stroke and less power; longer casts of over 40 feet require a longer stroke and more power.

Casting arch is the v-shaped arch between the rod in the start position and the rod in the stop position. This is where your rod tip starts and stops on the forward and back cast. Traditionally, these points are referred to by using the clock-face analogy, with twelve o'clock being directly overhead. On the basic cast we begin the stroke with our rod tip in the 2:00 position and end the stroke with our rod tip in the 10:00 position. Learning to keep your rod tip within these clock positions is a great starting point in practice, but keep an open mind. In actual casting situations, these rules will be frequently violated when we encounter obstacles to casting, such as trees, bushes or wind, or when we want to use different presentation techniques.

The casting arch, narrow or wide, is dependent on the size of the stroke and thus the power applied to the cast. Short strokes which require minimal power have narrow arcs, and long strokes, which require more power, have wider arcs. The position of your

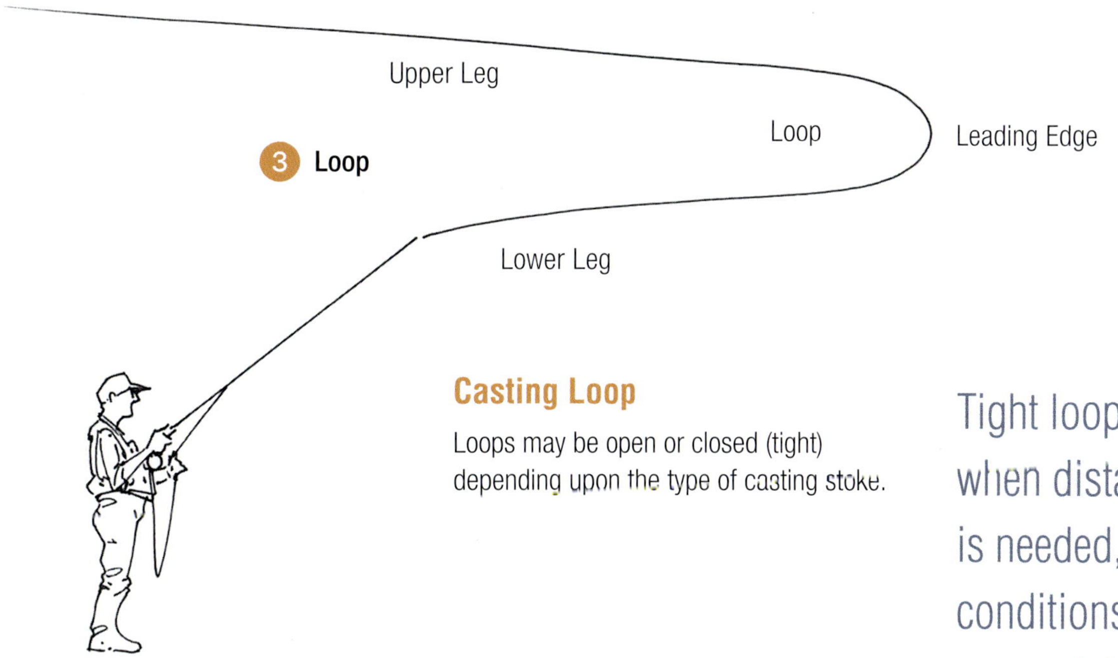

Casting Loop

Loops may be open or closed (tight) depending upon the type of casting stoke.

casting arch, either horizontal or perpendicular to the horizon, is determined by the position of your target and the type of casting you're doing.

Casting loops refers to the shape and path of the fly line as it "unrolls" through the air. Loops can be narrow, also called tight, or wide, also called open. Tight loops are useful when distance or accuracy is needed, or in windy conditions. Open loops are useful when casting weighted flies or multiple flies, so they don't catch the fly line or get tangled.

Tight loops are useful when distance or accuracy is needed, or in windy conditions. Open loops are useful when casting weighted flies or multiple flies, so they don't catch the fly line or get tangled.

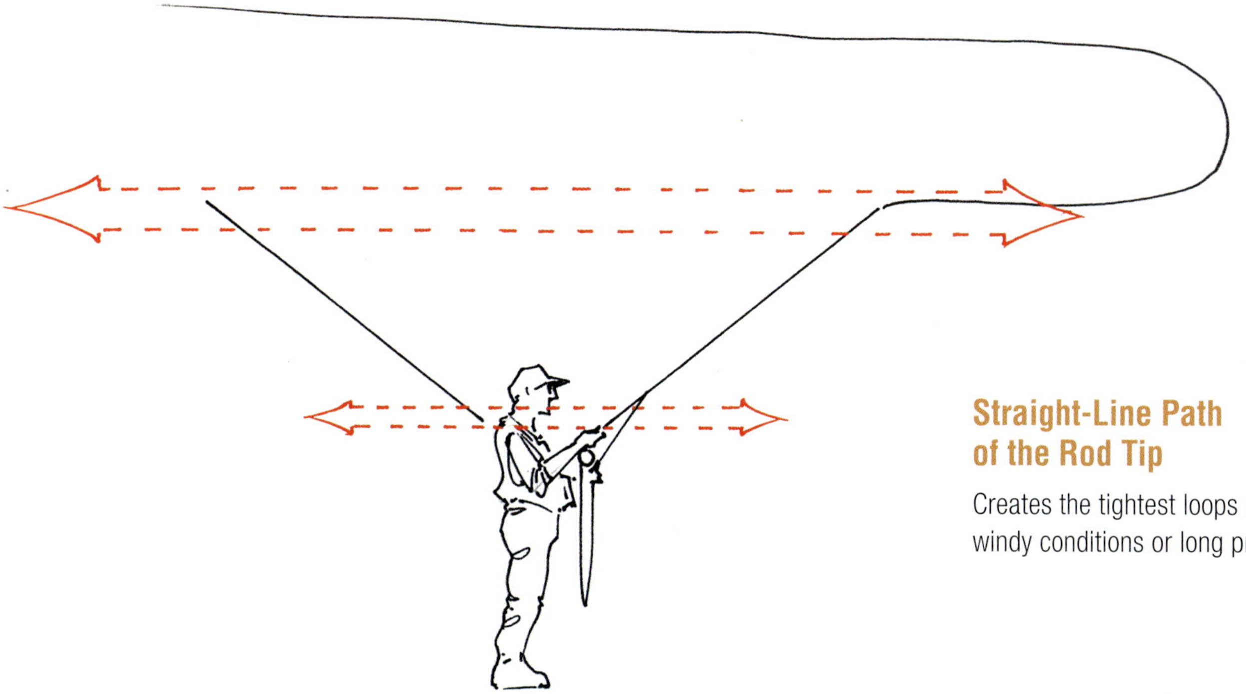

Straight-Line Path of the Rod Tip

Creates the tightest loops useful in windy conditions or long presentations.

Loop shapes are determined by the path of the rod tip, because the line will always follow the path of the rod tip. Moving the rod tip in a straight line will create a narrow loop; moving the rod tip in a convex path will create a wide loop; a concave path can occur when the rod is over powered, such that the rod tip dips below the path of the rod. A concave rod-tip path is never desirable and causes tailing loops. Loops are the key factor in determining accuracy, distance, presentation and line control.

Convex Path of a Rod Tip

A rounded rod tip path will create an open loop.

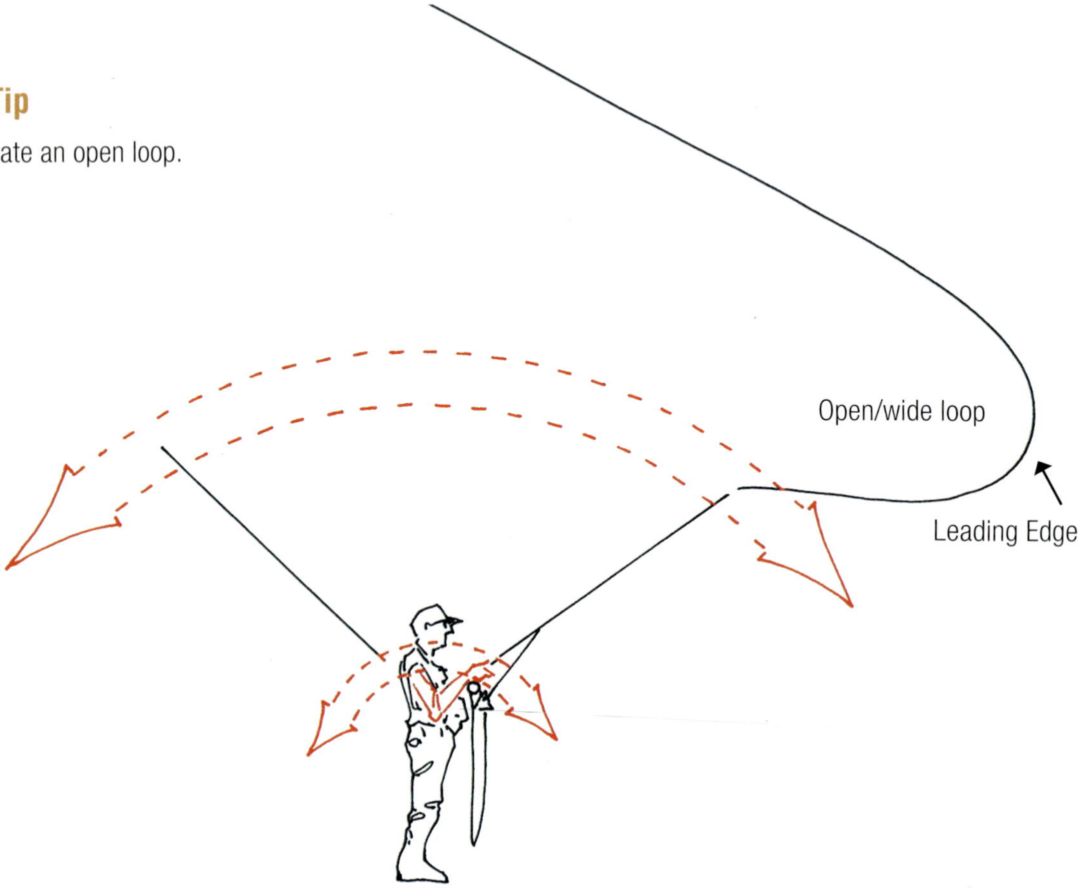

Concave Path of a Rod Tip

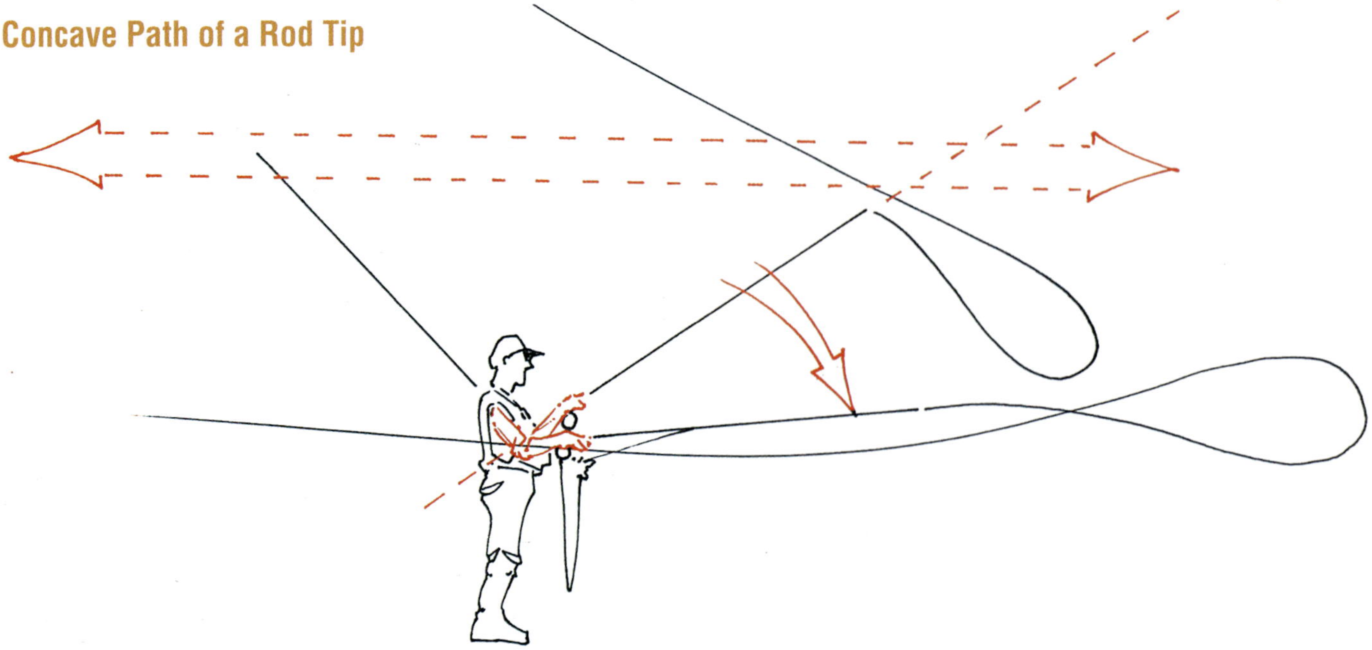

Federation of Flyfishers' Five Essentials of Fly Casting*

1 There must be a pause at the end of each stroke, which varies in duration with the amount of line beyond the rod tip.

Casting always has a tempo or rhythm which allows the line to straighten out on both the forward and back casts. Slack and a loss of power are created when the line is not allowed to straighten. Several problems can develop from this, such as hitting the water and failing to load the rod for the next stroke. The more line you are casting, the longer it takes for it to straighten out on each cast. The best way to learn what happens when the line straightens is to watch your casts on both the front and back stroke. You will see the line as it unfolds through the air, passing over your rod tip, and straightening out.

2 Slack line should be kept to an absolute minimum.

This is related to both picking-up the fly off the water and initiating your stroke. If there is no slack in your line, the fly will respond as soon as you move the line. When you pick your fly off the water, begin with your rod tip down low; slowly raise the rod tip taking up any slack in the line and begin your stroke. On the cast, wait for the line to straighten out before initiating your next cast.

3 During the casting stroke, the rod tip must travel in a straight-line path.

The caveat here is that this is what is required if you want to throw a tight loop, which is not always the case. However, the principle remains the same: the fly line will always follow the path of the rod tip. Moving the rod tip in a convex path will cause an open loop; a straight-line path will create a tight loop, and a concave path, where the tip dips below the path of the line will create tailing loops. Controlling how your rod tip travels is a matter of a controlled casting stroke and moving your hand in a straight-line path. Breaking your wrists, for example, during a cast will result in an automatic open loop.

4 The size of the casting arch must vary with the length of the line past the rod tip.

Short lines require a short stroke; long lines require a long stroke. Changing your stroke to adjust for the amount of line you're casting also changes the tempo of your cast, the trajectory or target, and the amount of power applied the cast.

5 Power must be applied in the proper amount at the proper place of power.

The stroke, or loading the rod, is initiated with a gradual acceleration leading to an abrupt stopping point (unloading the rod), which in our case occurs at the 10:00 and 2:00 positions). The abrupt stop is necessary to allow the transfer of energy to be applied to the fly line and carry it beyond the tip of the rod.

Brian Darnell

*Reprinted courtesy of the Gammel family and Federation of Flyfishers. To purchase a copy of their book, *Essentials of Fly Casting*, go to www.fedflyfishers.org and click on "Merchandise".

Placing your thumb on top of the handle will give you leverage needed to cast.

Grip

There are several grips, but the one most commonly used is similar to a handshake, the extended finger grip: the four fingers wrap the handle, with the index finger placed slightly above the lower three fingers, and the thumb rests on top of the handle. Placing your thumb on top of the handle will give you leverage needed to cast. The grip is the same one you use to cut with a knife, hold a screwdriver, or pick up something with a handle. *Practice this grip now.*

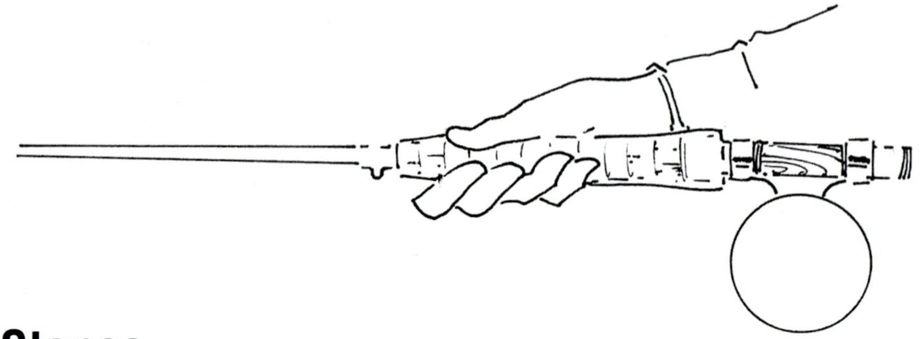

Gripping the Rod

The basic grip is similar to a handshake with thumb resting on top of the grip.

Stance

Stance is whatever is comfortable for you. Some casters use a forward-facing stance with their feet comfortably spaced and parallel. Other casters prefer a side-facing stance with their outside foot set forward of the inside foot. This latter stance is usually preferred when distance casting because it allows greater lateral movement of the arm and shoulder.

Hand, Arm and Wrist Position

Different casting styles emphasize different positions of the hand, arm and wrist. In this book I am going to advocate for a Mel Krieger style of casting which has the caster positioning the hand out in front and close to the shoulder. The wrist is straight and the elbow is at your side. The movement during the cast occurs in the arm and

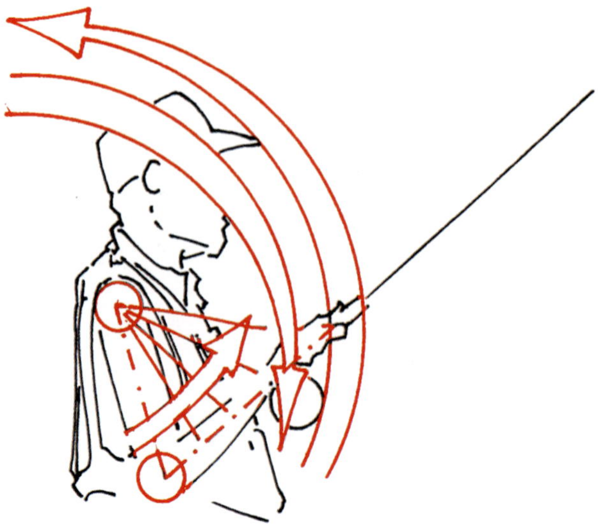

Basic Casting Stroke

Initiated with the use of the shoulder to lift (back cast) and pull down (forward cast). Wrist and forearm should remain locked, elbow near the body.

shoulder and can be thought of as a "lift or stab, and pull down." The lift, or back cast, is comparable to the action of stabbing a piece of wood directly above your head. The pull down, or forward cast, is like pulling down on a rope; your arm and shoulder guide your hand to the starting position. *Practice this action now.*

Line hand and rod hand work together. This angler has the line pinched under the finger of his rod hand as he strips in slack with his line hand.

Holding the Rod

The hand used to hold the rod is your rod hand; your other hand is your line hand and manages the slack line between the rod and reel. If there were no slack line off the reel then you could hold the line under the index finger on your rod hand and let your line hand free. The line hand, a real busybody in actual fishing conditions, is often the deciding factor in reaching your targets quickly and efficiently. In addition to holding the slack, the line hand manages casting distance by either tightening or releasing the slack on casts. In more advanced casting techniques, the line hand is used to increase the speed of the line, and it also strips in the line on almost all retrieve techniques. Learning to coordinate the actions of your line and rod hands will make you a better caster and more versatile angler.

Rod Hand and Line Hand

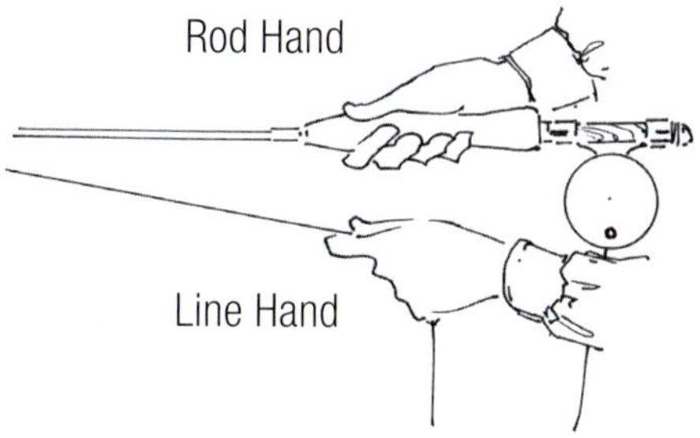

The Casts

Below, we learn several casts, including the basic cast. The principles and concepts discussed above apply to all these casts, so keep them in mind when you are reading or practicing.

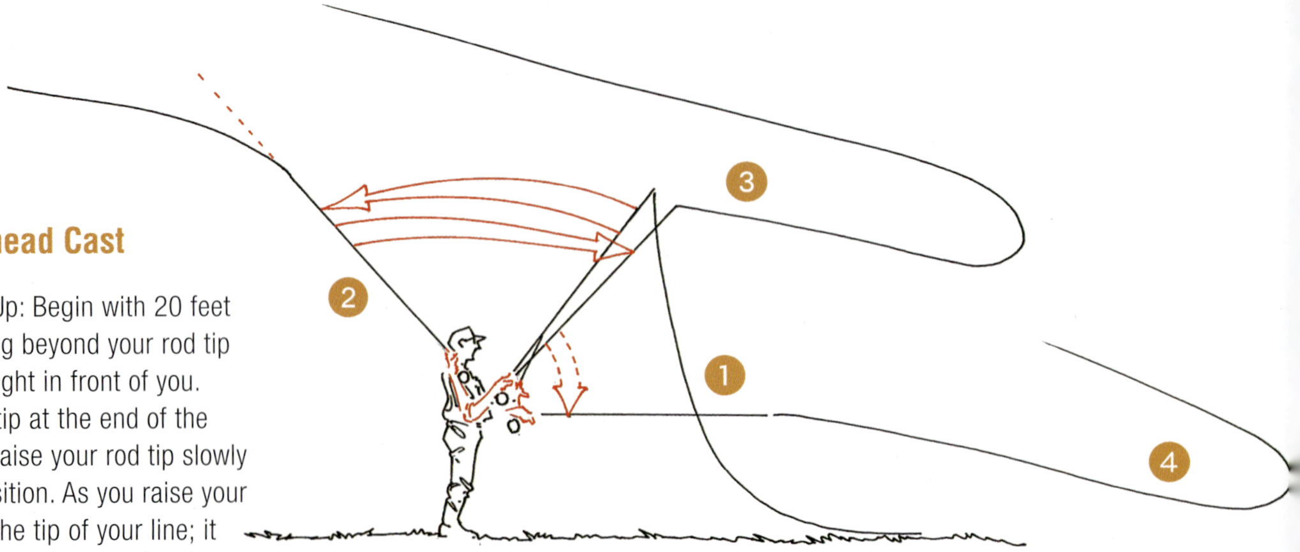

Basic Overhead Cast

1 The Pick-Up: Begin with 20 feet of line extending beyond your rod tip and laying straight in front of you. Point your rod tip at the end of the line, and then raise your rod tip slowly to the 2:00 position. As you raise your rod tip, watch the tip of your line; it should move if there is no slack in your line.

2 Back Stroke: Initiate your back cast with your rod tip starting at the 2:00 position. With a steady but quickening acceleration, pick up the line in front of you by moving the rod tip to the 10:00 position behind you (this is the lift). The tendency here is to move the rod off to the side for better leverage and power, which you will want to do with longer casts. But with a shorter cast, try and keep the rod in front of you such that it almost feels like you're going to hit your nose or brush your ear with your rod hand. This action will keep your rod tip high behind you. Ideally, you want to feel as if you are throwing the tip of your rod to the top of a tree.

3 Forward Stroke: With your rod tip in the 10:00 position and the fly line straightened out behind you, move your arm back to the starting position (this is the pull-down) with your rod tip ending in the 2:00 position and the line directly in front of you.

4 Lay Down: This is the opposite of the pick-up in step one. With your rod tip in the 2:00 position simply lower your rod tip and point it at the end of the fly line. This drops your line back down on the water.

Overhead Cast

The overhead cast is the most basic cast in fly-fishing. Often referred to as the dry-fly cast, it is composed of four parts: the pick-up, back stroke, forward stroke and lay down. For clarity, we will break up the cast into its disparate parts, but in practice, all four steps are linked together in a continuous movement. If done correctly, this cast should end with your line positioned straight out in front of you as you started. If you want to false cast, repeat steps two and three in succession without letting the line touch the ground. First try practicing this cast without fly line to get the feel of how your arm should move the rod. Then add fly line when you feel confident.

Water-Load Cast

As the name implies, this cast uses the surface tension of the water to load the rod on both the forward and back cast. All we are doing is releasing that power at the end of our stroke so that the line straightens out.

The sequences of events in this cast are: pick-up, back cast, lay down; pick-up, forward cast, lay down. The only thing that changes between this cast and the basic cast is we are laying the fly line on the water after each stroke. No false casting is involved.

This is a useful cast in windy conditions when false casting may be difficult, or when you want to shoot line with one stroke. The main criterion for this cast is that you have enough water both behind and in front of you, and there is no slack in the line between the rod tip and the fly. You may also water-load in just one direction and complete the rest of the cast as normal.

Follow the exact steps for the basic cast, except you lay your line onto the water after each stroke on both the forward and back casts.

Water-Load Cast

Best used when needing to pick-up your fly and shoot it back out into the water with one or two false casts.

1. Draw the line out of the water to start your casting arch.
2. Make a normal back cast.
3. Make a normal forward cast.

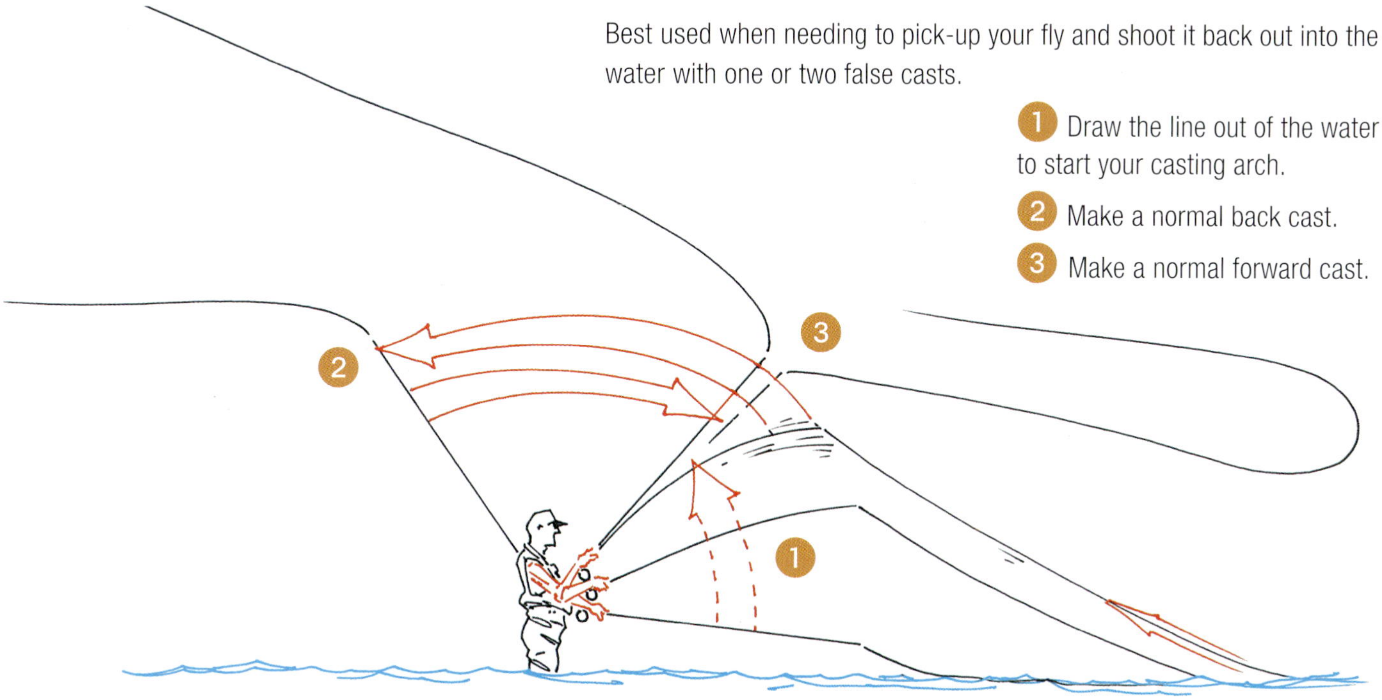

Craig Schuhmann

Because big fish are wary, stealth is often required. Learn to apply a variety of casts and presentation techniques to improve your chances.

Roll Cast

Other than the basic cast, the roll cast is the most intuitive of all casts. If you never took a casting lesson or read this book, but fished a lot, you would eventually figure out this cast.

There are going to be times when a back cast is not possible because of brush, trees, or other obstacles behind you. How, then, do you get the line out in front of you? The roll cast is a useful way to pick up line and deliver a cast in front of you when a back cast is not possible. The steps of this cast are: pick-up, stop, forward cast. The roll cast is a variation of a water-load cast because we need the surface tension of the water to help load the rod on the forward cast.

Mel Krieger compares this stroke to the action required for sticking a meat cleaver or hatchet into a chopping block, with the similar abrupt stop that would happen once the hatchet hits the block. If done right you should see the line roll out in front of you.

Roll Cast

Useful when a back cast is not possible or to pick a fly up off the water quickly.

1 Pick-Up: Ensuring there is no slack in the line, pick up your rod tip as in the basic cast but move it up and behind you at approximately the 10:00 or 11:00.

2 Stop: Stop the rod at this point but only for a few seconds (seems a bit long) in actual practice. Most of the fly line will be in front of you, but sliding towards you with the line coming out of the rod tip at your side (it's at my side?), this is referred to as a "D" loop. Once the line stops sliding, you are ready to begin your forward stroke.

3 Forward Stroke: Same as the basic cast, initiate your forward stroke or pull down. However, because you are lifting a portion of line off the water, your stroke needs to be quicker and more forceful than a regular stroke to load the rod.

Presentation Casts

Presentation casts are variations of the basic cast, and each has its usefulness in specific fishing situations that I will highlight under each description. The proper cast to use is determined by how you choose to present a fly; this, in turn, depends on variables such as water speed, water type, current lanes, obstacles, and your position to the fish. All of these casts are used to manipulate the fly line, not the fly, because it is the behavior of the fly line on the water which allow our fly to appear naturally to the trout.

Straight-Line Cast

A straight-line cast ends with a straight-line connection to the fly. On the final forward cast, aim just above the water, soften your stroke just a touch so there is no bounce-back, and drop the rod tip (and thus the line) to the water.

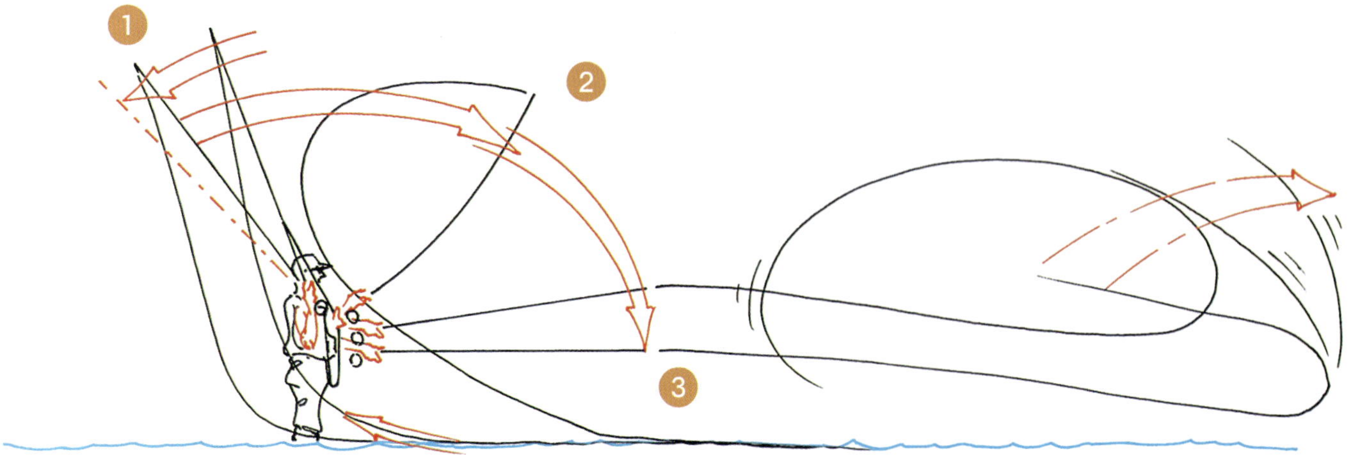

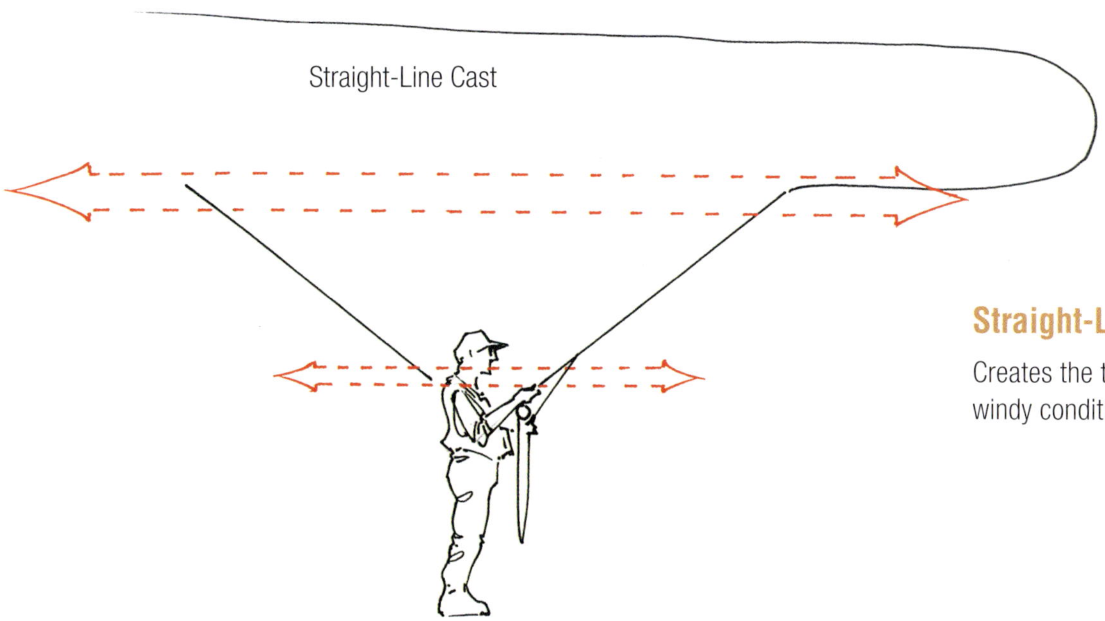

Straight-Line Cast

Creates the tightest loops useful in windy conditions or long presentations.

Actual uses of a straight-line cast are limited to a few specific fishing situations. An angler may use a straight-line cast when fishing from a boat; when moving with the current; when streamer or wet-fly fishing and the presentation is downstream; when a quick retrieve is needed, such as in an upstream cast; or when fishing on a lake.

Slack-Line Casts

Slack-line casts are executed to reduce water current drag on the fly. This cast is useful when fishing dry flies, nymph fishing and some streamer-fishing presentations. Slack-line casts also enable the angler to feed slack line into a drift without disturbing the position of the fly on the water.

These are the most useful casts in fly-fishing because we are rarely in a situation where all river currents are even. We need to anticipate pull on the line that can reduce the natural drift of the fly. The bounce, wiggle cast or s-curve, pile, and reach cast are four examples of slack-line casts.

Bounce Cast

Cast as you would with the basic cast, but on the final forward cast the line is stopped abruptly 2-3 feet above the water so there is a recoil effect. The recoil places slack (in the form of waves) in the line which, when dropped to the water, allows the fly to drift freely.

This cast is useful when fishing dry flies or casting over multiple current lanes. It is also useful for getting a drag-free drift in difficult situations such as a downstream presentation with a dry fly.

1 Stop the rod suddenly on your final forward cast.

2 Pull the rod back slightly before letting the line hit the water.

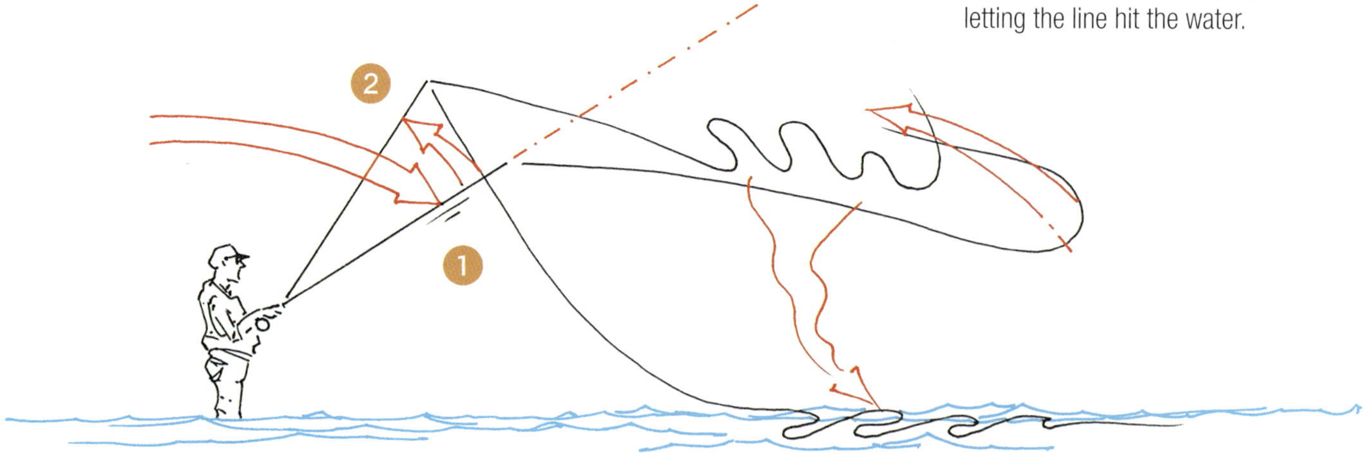

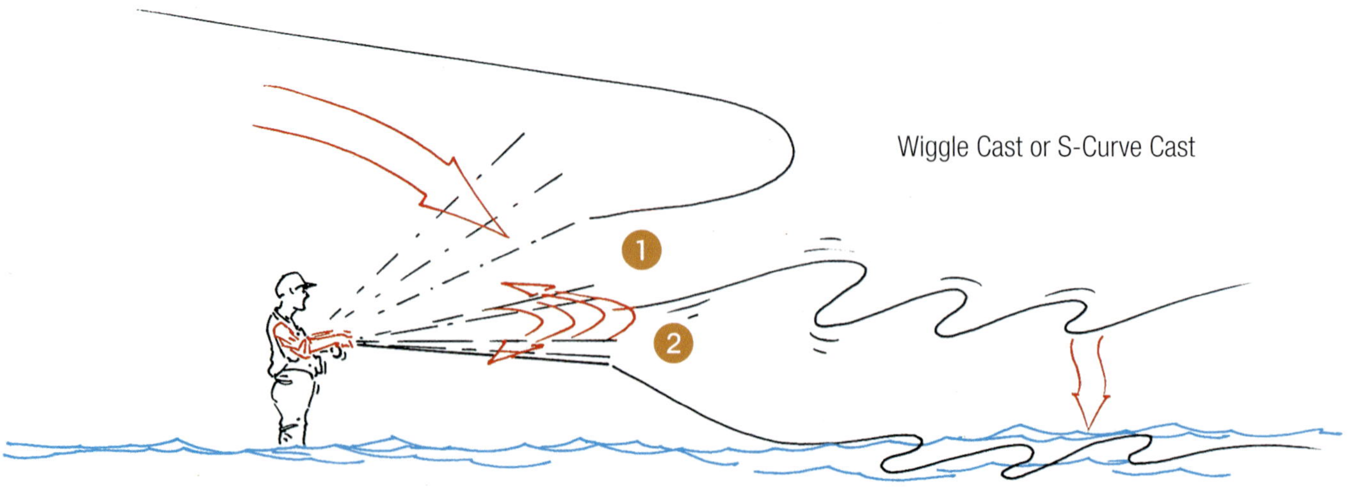

Wiggle Cast or S-Curve Cast

Using the basic cast, on the final forward cast the rod tip is wiggled and the line is dropped to the water. The wiggle will place S-curves in the line, allowing enough slack to give a drag-free drift.

Also useful when fishing dry flies or fishing over multiple current lanes.

1. Make your final forward cast.
2. Wiggle the rod tip back and forth quickly just before dropping your line to the water.

Pile Cast

The pile cast puts slack in your line for a drag-free drift similar to the bounce cast and wiggle cast.

On the final forward cast, project the line up towards the tree-tops and drop the rod tip to the water; this will result in the line near the fly piling up into a mess of slack.

This cast is useful where faster currents lie between the caster and the fish.

1. Make final forward cast with a high trajectory.
2. With line still high in the air, move your rod tip quickly to the water surface resulting in the line falling to the water in a pile.

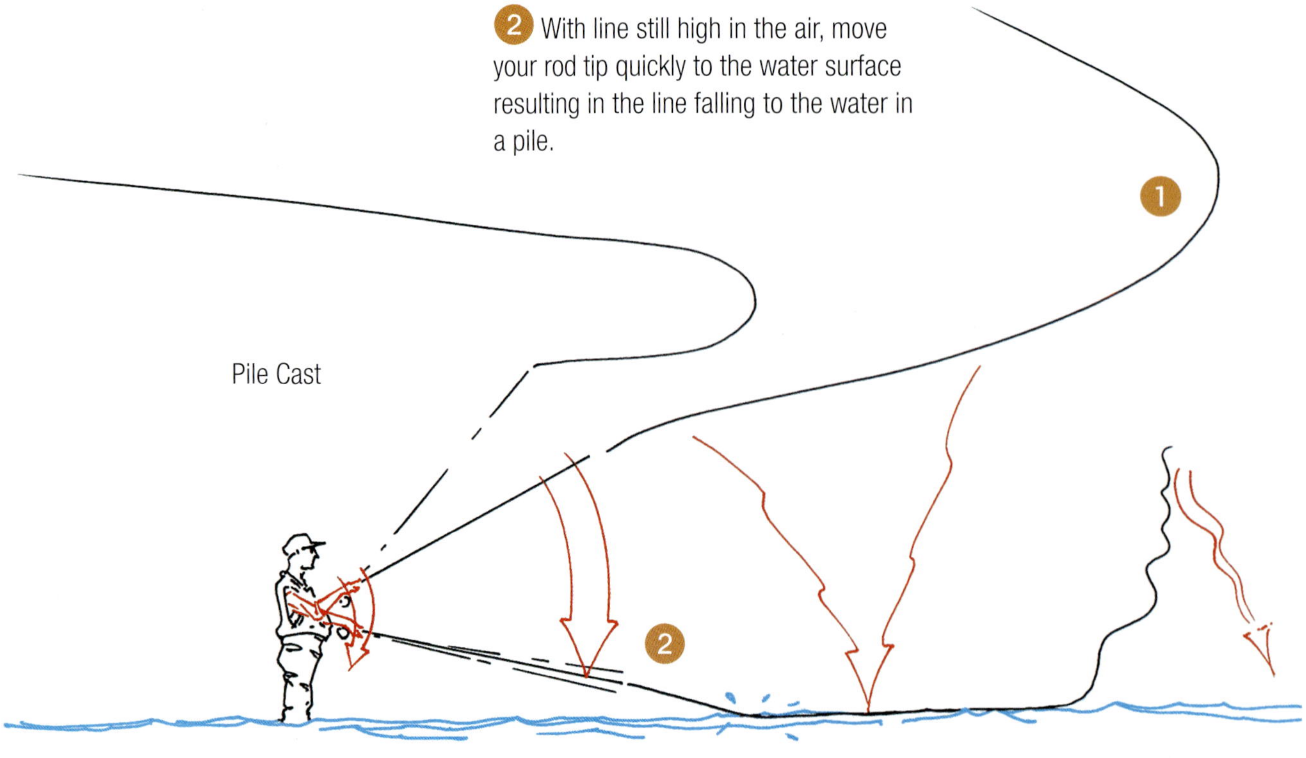

Good anglers will bend forward as they watch intently the drift of the fly, prepared to detect even the subtlest strike.

Reach Cast

On the final forward cast, the rod tip is positioned quickly to the upstream side of the angler. This is a useful cast when fishing across or down and across stream currents and for getting an extended drift with a side-stream presentation. When executed properly, the reach places the fly line above or across from the fly, allowing the line to drift for a ways before pulling on the fly.

1. Make your final forward cast.
2. Prior to the line hitting the water, move your whole arm down and to the side to position the rod tip upstream and lay your line on the water.

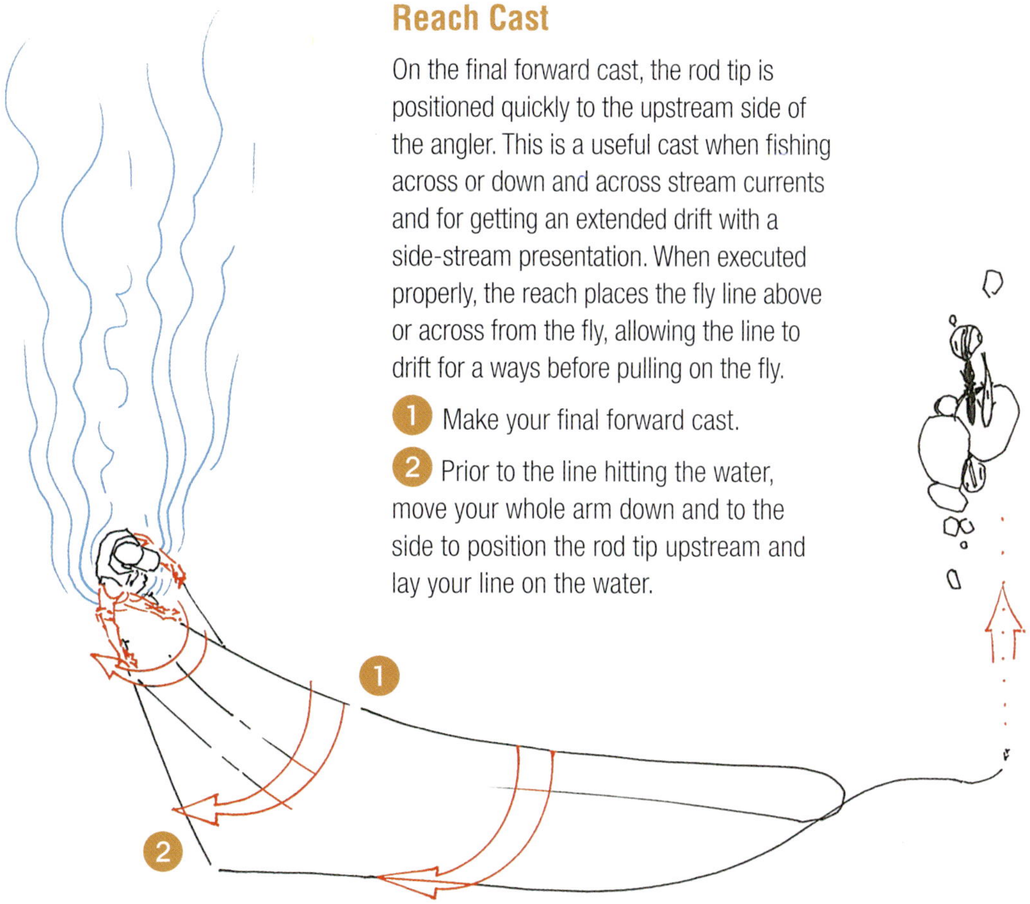

Positive and Negative Curve Casts

Of all the fly-fishing casts, I use these the least because I just don't find a lot of situations which demand angled casts. I'm much more likely to reposition myself to get an easier angle on the fish. Also, line control with these casts is often difficult. These casts are used to place a fly around obstacles or position a fly to the right or left of the fly line, such as in upstream dry-fly fishing.

To throw a positive curve cast, tilt your rod tip off to the side and make a side-arm cast. On your final stroke, simply overpower the cast; leader tippet and fly should kick to the left.

The negative curve cast can be made in one of two ways: Casting over your opposite shoulder with the same overpowered side-arm cast, or using a regular side-arm cast, under power your cast.

A common adage among fly-anglers is: "No mend, no bend."

Casting Problems and How to Fix Them

Casting is about line control and being able to achieve the distance, accuracy and presentation to get the fly to the fish. All casting faults can be traced to the casting stroke, and thus to the way the caster is moving the rod. Remember, the fly line follows the path of the rod tip. To solve these problems we must first look at what the line is doing, then understand what the rod is doing, and finally what the caster is doing.

Problem: Fly Line Piling Up in Front of You

Cause: Open loops that result from a wide arching path of the rod tip. In all cases, this problem is caused by breaking the wrists on the back cast and/or dropping our tip on the forward cast.

Solution: Avoid breaking your wrist on the back cast. Rather, use your arm and shoulder to lift the rod tip and bring it back down.

Problem: Slapping the Water on the Forward Cast

Causes: Open loops which do not allow the line to flatten out in front of the caster, and too low of a trajectory. In the first instance, the line will pile up in front of the caster, which results in slapping the water. In the second, the caster is not aiming the cast above the water or target.

Solution: Flatten the casting arch by not breaking the wrists, and aim the fly above the water or the target. Here it is important to think about your target and where you want the fly to go. Without a specific target in mind we are apt to cast randomly and with little control.

Problem: Hitting the Water Behind You

Cause: Open loops caused by a wide arching path of the rod tip. Similar to the problem above, the caster is breaking the wrist and dropping the rod tip.

Solution: Use the arm and shoulder to lift the rod and maintain a high rod-tip position on the back cast.

Problem: Knots in the Leader or Fly Line, Sometimes Referred to as Wind Knots

Causes: Not allowing the line to straighten on each cast, or overpowering the cast.

Solution: Allow sufficient time for the line to straighten out on each cast; maintain a smooth acceleration in the casting stroke so as not to overpower the rod.

Problem: The Line Will Not Go Out

Causes: Failure to load the rod and releasing line at the wrong time.

Solution: This problem is related to the application of power during the cast and feeding line into the cast to achieve distance. In order to properly load the rod there must be enough fly line beyond the rod tip, and the rod must be stopped with enough force at the end of each cast. At minimum, one should have 20-30 feet of line beyond the rod tip to begin loading the rod. Line should only be released into the cast at the end of each stroke when the rod is unloading. Releasing line during the stroke takes away from the power applied to the rod during the cast, and the cast will collapse into a jumbled mess.

The ring of the rise.

Suggestions for Casting Practice

Setting aside time to practice off the water can greatly improve your casting skills. Practice only works when we are not distracted with trying to catch fish.

Always attach a leader to your fly line to prevent damaging the end of your fly line.

- ✓ Find a large grassy area with room for both forward and back casts.
- ✓ Always attach a leader to your fly line to prevent damaging the end of your fly line. Do not use a real fly. Instead, tie a piece of colored yarn at the end of your leader.
- ✓ Set up targets: Setting up a target will help with accuracy and give you a goal. Set targets at distances of 15, 30, 45, and 60 feet. Your goals are to reach the target and place the fly in the center of the target.
- ✓ Position yourself so you can watch your back cast and forward cast. This will help you with timing because you can see how long it takes for your line to straighten out before initiating each stroke.
- ✓ Cast with a friend or experienced angler and ask for feedback.
- ✓ Ignore smart comments from passersby who are more than happy to tell you that fish can't be caught on land.
- ✓ Enjoy yourself. A lot of anglers get great pleasure from the casting itself.

Trees, as well as high grass or brush can make casting difficult at best. Knowing a variety of casts, such as the roll cast, will help you overcome these difficulties.

6

Trout Flies, Insects, & Other Food Forms

The first question all beginning anglers ask is, "which fly do I use?" Indeed, this is the question that opens the door to the totality of our sport, and all our theories about why trout take our flies at all. Approaches to this question have ranged from the single-fly theory to very complex "match the hatch" ideologies. The truth of course lies somewhere in-between, and what I hope to do in this chapter is to get you thinking about flies and their importance to the angler and the fish. We will also learn how artificial flies relate to the actual insects and aquatic food forms they represent. This information will give you a firm foundation to learn more detailed and nuanced information as you develop as a fly-angler.

First let's consider for a moment the observations of two notable anglers on the topic of flies. In 1964 angling writer Roderick Haig-Brown wrote, "the first important thing to realize about artificial flies for all types of fishing is that there are far too many patterns . . . the type of fly and how and where it's fished will always be of far greater importance than the exact pattern."

A similar sentiment is echoed by a more contemporary writer, Denny Rickards, who advises anglers to think "beyond the fly" as the key to catching trout, and consider presentation, tackle, times and places we choose to fish, as well as the habits of trout, as clues for consistently catch trout.

Denny places emphasis on fly lines and claims to change fly lines more than some anglers change flies.

He says, "Too often we change flies assuming the fish are looking for something different, when the real problem is that we're using a line that's not presenting the fly where the fish are feeding."

Both men reduce the emphasis on the fly, in favor of presentation or the method with which the fly is fished. Neither would deny that the right fly is also important, particularly with dry flies, but over time a well-fished fly, regardless of the type of fly, will catch more fish than the right fly.

Later in the chapter you will see a list of commonly accepted flies that have proven themselves over time and will catch fish anywhere. These flies are called "attractor" patterns and their primary effectiveness comes from being general. They do not represent anything in particular but the types and arrangement of materials on these flies are effective for catching most trout.

Before you start fishing a particular river or stream, it's wise to supplement the list of attractors with "local preferences." These are flies that have proven themselves effective in a specific area

Begin by noticing the presence of certain streamside insects, such as this mayfly, and associating them with earlier or later stages of development such as nymphs, spinners, or emergers.

and are obtained from a local fly shop or angler. As you get more comfortable with a broad range of flies and how to use them, you may want to get more specific, studying the specific insects on the streams you fish and developing a "match the hatch" technique that works for you.

There are two basic fly types: dry and wet, or surface and subsurface.

Types of Flies

There are two basic fly types: dry and wet, or surface and subsurface. These designations relate not to the type of fly being fished, but the method with which they are used. Many anglers have adapted dry flies to wet-fly fishing and vice versa.

Dry flies float on the water and, depending on their size, will be visible to the angler. Dry-fly fishing is what most people think of when they think of fly-fishing, because it is the most visual form of

Fly selection does not have to be complicated. Attractor patterns such as Parachute Adams or Pheasant Tail Nymphs can be fished on any river with great success.

Tomette Schuhmann

fishing: we see the fly drifting along the current and we see the fish break the surface of the water to eat the fly.

Wet flies, on the other hand, are fished below the surface, and in most cases we see neither fish nor fly. The whole event of the strike is hidden until we feel the pull of the fish on the line. This method was long thought to be an inferior method, lacking the need for skill simply because the strike was never seen, but today wet-fly fishing is considered by many anglers to be the more demanding of the two approaches.

The Muddler Minnow created by Don Gapen of Anoka, Minnesota in 1937 is a highly versatile fly, fished dry or wet, and a standard selection for many of today's anglers.

Within these two basic categories, there are five types of flies: dry fly, nymph, wet fly, emerger and streamer. "Wet fly" in this list refers to a specific type of fly and should not be confused with all flies fished subsurface. Within each type, there is a vast array of patterns and styles to choose from, and this can sometimes be confusing and overwhelming to the beginning angler.

A fly pattern is defined as a certain arrangement of fur, feathers, tinsel and other materials on a hook and suggests a range of hook sizes and colors. The "style" of the fly suggests further changes in the pattern such that the same fly may look different depending upon the style. For instance (and don't worry about remembering these names right now!) an Adams, a gray-colored dry fly, can be tied in the traditional Catskill or parachute style. Some mayfly patterns such as Blue Winged Olives and Pale Morning Duns come tied in a greater range of styles such as the two mentioned above, or perhaps a Compara-dun, or no-hackle style. The diversity of fly styles and patterns was developed to meet a variety of stream types and fishing conditions.

Hook Sizes

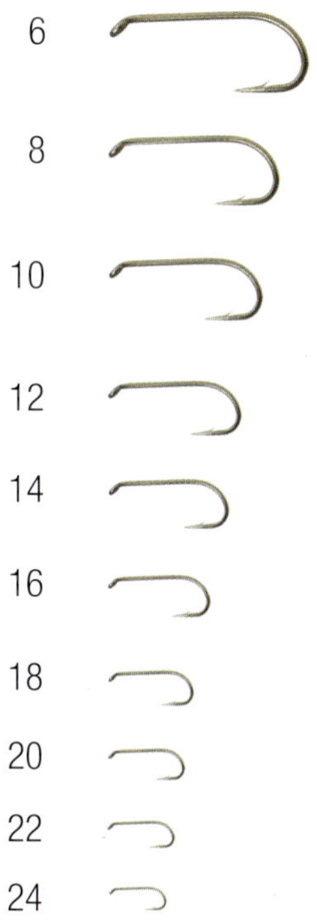

The theory behind fly design is simple: Approximate the size, shape, color, and movement of the actual insect or food form. These four basic elements, listed in order of importance, are thought to trigger the fish's reaction to either reject or accept a fly.

The size of the fly is based on hook size. The size of the fly you fish can be important, especially if fish are being selective. Hooks come in many shapes and sizes, and the larger the number the smaller the hook. Thus, a size 26 is a very small hook and a size 2 is quite large. Hook sizes between 18 and 6 are the most common for trout fishing. In this range you can match most trout food-forms, whether you are fishing dry flies, streamers, or nymphs.

Are there exceptions to the size, shape, color and movement formula of flies, such that a fish may eat a fly that bears little resemblance to the insect or food form it is eating? Absolutely! And the diversity of exceptions that come from anglers' experiences are vast. For this reason, flies are generally broken down into two categories: Attractors and imitators.

The former is based on a simple principle: Fish feed opportunistically, so anything that is put in the fish's field of view will be considered or rejected based on its appearance and attractive qualities.

Attractor flies are nonspecific in size, shape and color and don't represent anything in particular.

Many subsurface attractor patterns emphasize movement over size, shape, and color as a key quality. Such is the case with the Woolly Bugger which can represent any number of fast-swimming food forms, such as a leech, large nymph or baitfish imitation. Attractor dry flies such as the Royal Wulff tend to emphasize shape or silhouette over size and color. The Royal Wulff distinguishes itself from other natural insects by sharing the components of many insects on the water. Thus, a Royal Wulff can be fished over any number of different insect hatches. Other examples of attractor flies are the Zonker, Humpy, Adams, and Madam X.

The latter group of flies, imitators, represents the opposing side of fish behavior. The principle here is selectivity. That is, fish will reject anything that does not closely mimic, in size, shape and color, the exact food it is feeding on. These latter flies come from a school of fly-fishing called Matching the Hatch. Matching the Hatch is a technical approach to fly selection and is rooted in entomology, the scientific study of insects. Examples of imitative flies are the Blue Winged Olive Compara-dun, Pale Morning Dun No Hackle, Trico Biot Spinner, and extended-body mayflies.

Traditional Catskill Dry Fly

The large hackle and tail made of stiff hackle fibers enable this fly to float high on the surface of the water.

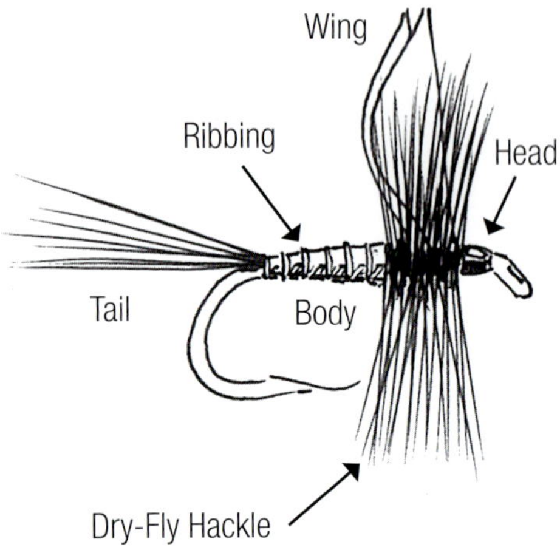

Basic Style Nymph

Hare's Ears and Pheasant Tail Nymphs will have this shape which shows a taper from the head to the tail. Compared with actual nymphs this basic shape is highly representative.

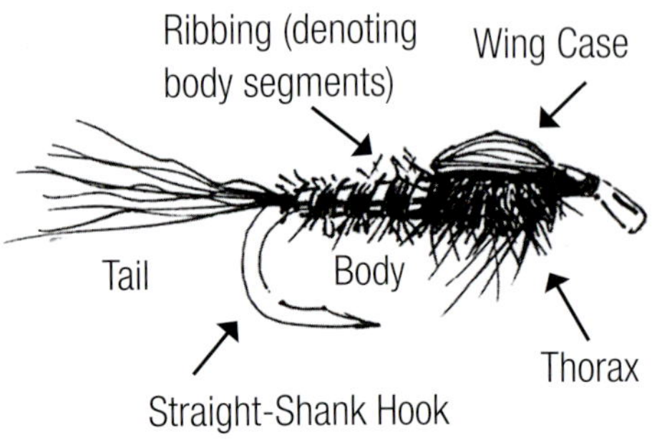

The Flies

Dries

Dry flies imitate the adult stage of aquatic and terrestrial insects when the insect is floating on the surface of the water as either a newly emerged insect or an insect that has returned to the water to die or lay eggs. Dry flies are constructed with materials that are buoyant, such as deer and elk hair, foam, and other water-shedding synthetic materials, and they are dressed with appropriate oils or grease to facilitate floatation. Examples of dry flies are the Elk Hair Caddis, Parachute Adams, Royal Wulff, and Humpy; grasshopper, ant and beetle patterns.

Nymphs

Nymphs represent the immature stages of an aquatic insect and are always fished subsurface. Nymph patterns are often weighted, constructed of materials that absorb water, and with fewer materials (sparsely constructed) to enable sinking. Examples of nymphs are the Hare's Ear, Pheasant Tail, and Copper John.

Emergers

These flies represent the emerging adult or nymph as it struggles in the surface film to emerge as an adult. Emerger patterns are tied without weight, with materials allowing it to suspend just below the surface. Think of emergers as a cross between a nymph and a dry fly. Examples of emergers include cripples, stillborn patterns and floating nymphs.

Wet Flies

Wet flies are a specific category of fly not to be confused with all flies fished subsurface. Fished subsurface, wet flies represent various adult or emerging insects, drowned adults, or returning adults that dive under the water to lay eggs. Common wet flies include soft-hackled flies, winged soft hackles, wingless wets and flymphs.

Streamers

Streamers are fished subsurface and represent baitfish, leeches, large swimming nymphs such as damsels, crayfish, and even mice. Streamers are constructed on larger hooks with materials such as natural or synthetic hairs that give the appearance of a streamlined, swift-darting object. The most common streamer is the Woolly Bugger, followed by the Muddler and Zonker.

The Insects

In order to understand how artificial flies relate to the insects and aquatic food forms they represent, we need to understand these food forms, have some idea of their lifecycle, and when and how they are available to trout.

There are five basic food forms available to trout: mayflies, caddis, stoneflies, terrestrials, and miscellaneous (leeches, freshwater crustaceans, and water beetles). Within each form, there is a great diversity in species size, shape, color, and behavior, but these can be generalized for a basic understanding. There are three other types of insects which we will not discuss because they are more commonly associated with lake fishing: cranefly, damsels, and midges.

All insects go through various stages of metamorphous from egg to adult. A vast majority of these insects are waterborne, spending most of their lifecycle in the habitat of trout. Thus, trout feed on these insects at various stages in the insect's lifecycle. When we speak of an insect hatch, we are referring to the time when insects emerge from an immature stage to the adult stage, resulting most often in the appearance of the insect on the surface of the water, in the air or on land.

Let's take a more in-depth look at the five basic food forms.

Mayflies

Anglers are deeply attracted to mayflies, the most loved of all aquatic insects, not only for their importance to fish, but also for their graceful and delicate beauty, and the fact that most mayfly hatches

Emerger Style Fly

A curved hook is common on emerger patterns to denote the swimming or kicking action of an emerging insect.

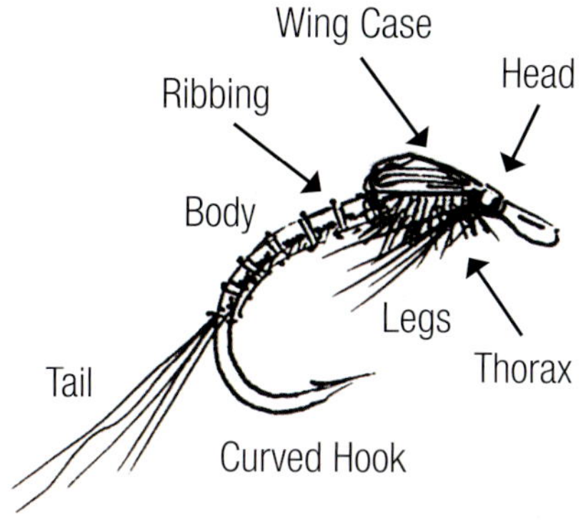

Soft-Hackle Fly

A soft-hackle fly is denoted by long webby hackle that extends from the head of the fly to beyond the bend of the hook.

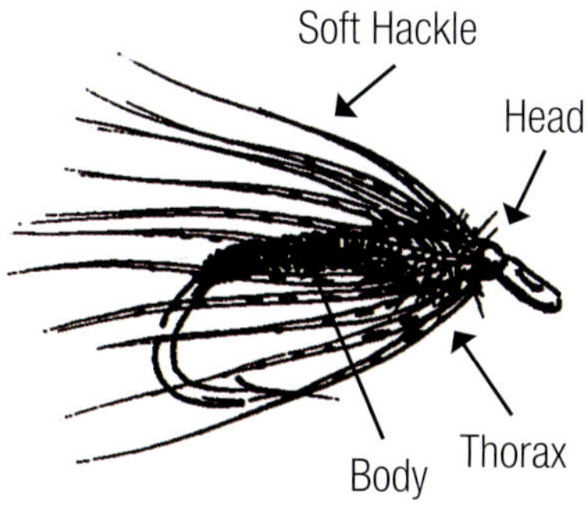

Streamers

Elongated, sleek appearance with many moving parts in the form of a long marabou tail and webby hackle. Long appearance resembles the swimming action of small baitfish, leeches, and larger swimming nymphs.

Mayfly nymphs are available to trout most of the time, whereas adults are only available during a hatch.

are fished with visible dry flies. Mayflies can be found in great diversity in almost every body of water.

Fish are very aware of their presence and feed on mayflies regularly throughout the year, but they are not always the most important food form to trout. The most important food forms to trout are those that are most abundant, and mayflies can be a fickle bunch of insects with sporadic availability and hatch times.

All adult mayflies have a basic form that any angler can easily learn to identify. The tell-tale features are upright wings, slender curving body and two or three tails. Common colors include shades of olive, yellow, green, brown, gray, yellow and black. Sizes range from very small, the head of a pin, to very large, the size of a half dollar. Mayfly nymphs can be harder to distinguish from other insect forms; making this distinction often requires some entomology background.

Mayflies have what is called an incomplete metamorphosis; that is, they have three stages of development: egg, nymph and adult. At the time of emergence, some nymphs begin a migration to the streamside, where they crawl out onto landforms such as rocks, grass and logs and hatch into adults. Others emerge from their nymphal stage along the bottom of the river and emerge to the surface as adults. Still other nymphs swim to the surface and emerge into adults, crawling out of their nymphal skins (also called shucks).

Once the nymph becomes an adult, it leaves the stream environment to molt into a sexually mature adult and begin mating. This is when you may find mayflies clustered on streamside vegetation such as trees, bushes and grass, a quick inspection of these areas will tell you if there is a hatch in progress.

A sexually mature mayfly is called a spinner. In this stage the mayflies mate, then the female returns to the water to deposit her eggs and die on the water surface. This final stage of the mayfly's life is called a spinner fall and can produce some of the best fishing for fly-anglers.

Mayfly nymphs are available to trout most of the time, whereas adults are only available during a hatch. For this reason, imitating the nymphs often produces the best fishing, and it pays to know a little about how the various mayfly nymphs live in the water.

Behaviorally, mayfly nymphs are divided into four categories: swimmers, crawlers, clingers and burrowers.

Mayfly Life Cycle

Mayflies are an important food source for trout. There are many fly patterns that match various stages of the insect's development, including nymphs, emergers, adults, and spinners. Develop a knowledge of these fly patterns and how to use them.

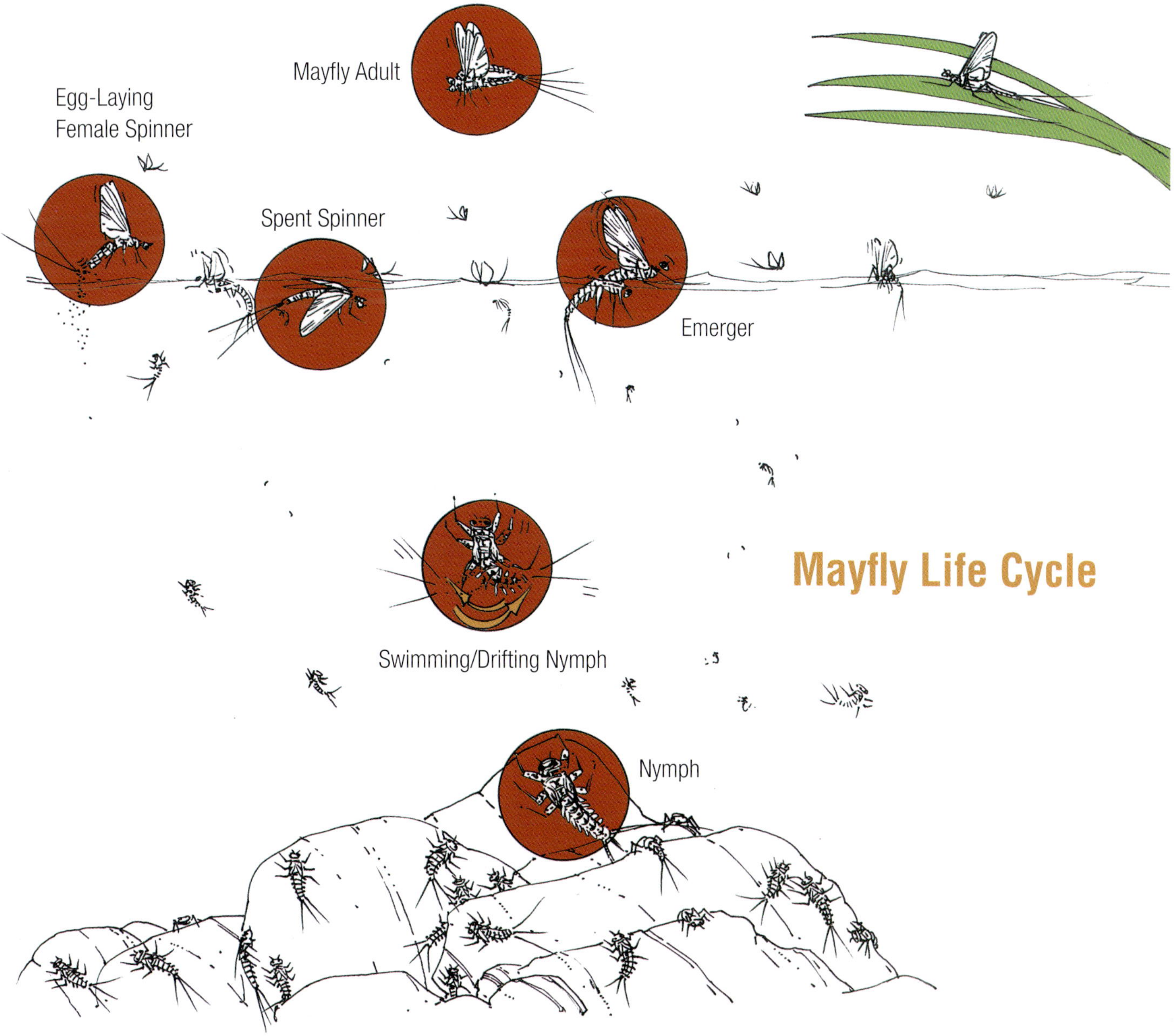

Swimmer mayflies are narrowly shaped and spend their life darting here and there like small minnows, among rocks and other obstacles. Examples of swimmer nymphs are *Baetis*, or blue-winged olives.

Clinger mayflies are flat, muscular nymphs adapted to fast-water environments. Clingers live on stream-bottom structure such as rocks and logs and use small suction cups to prevent being washed into the current. Examples of clingers are green drakes.

Crawlers have rounded, tapered bodies and are adapted to slower currents where they crawl around the vegetation feeding on river debris. Crawlers are also terrible swimmers and when washed into the current are helpless against predators. Examples of crawlers are pale morning duns and *Tricos*.

Burrowers have long slender bodies and live most of their life buried in the soft substrata of river bottoms. Burrowers are strong swimmers, most available to fish when they emerge from their burrows to emerge in the surface film. Examples of burrowers are big yellow mayflies (*Hexagenia*) and brown drakes.

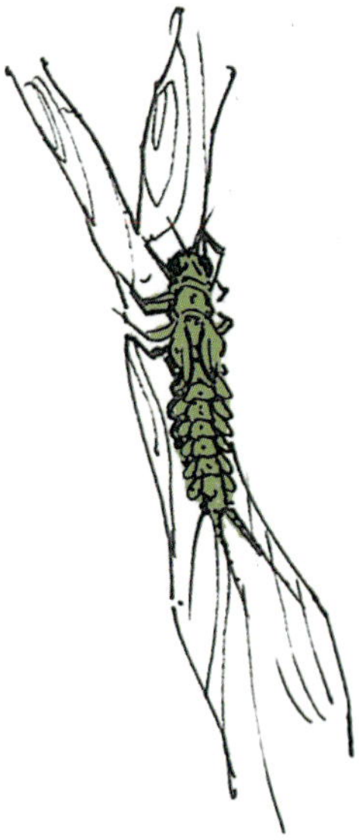

Swimmer Mayfly Nymphs

Swimmer mayflies are narrowly shaped and spend their life darting here and there like small minnows, among rocks and other obstacles. Examples of swimmer nymphs are *Baetis*, or blue-winged olives.

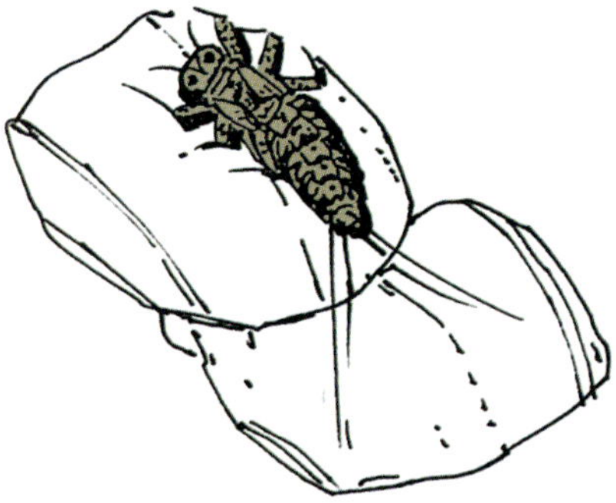

Clinger Mayfly Nymphs

Clinger mayflies are flat, muscular nymphs adapted to fast-water environments. Clingers live on stream-bottom structures such as rocks and logs and use small suction cups to prevent being washed into the current. Examples of clingers are green drakes.

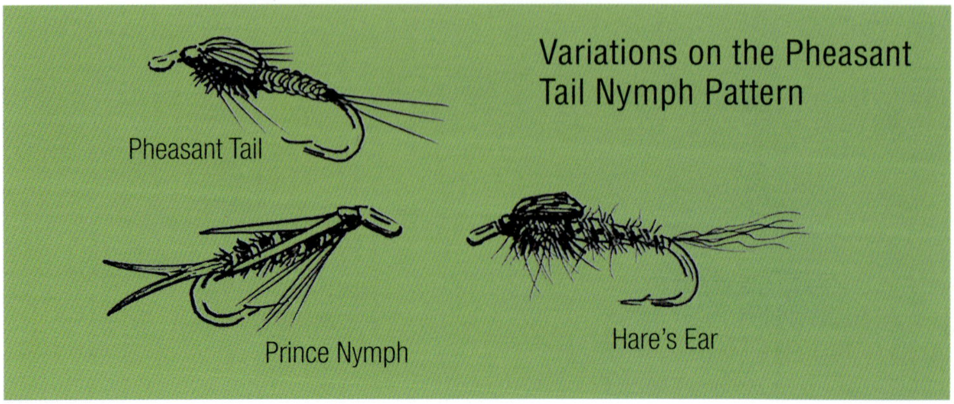

Craig Schuhmann

Insect hatches, such as this black drake hatch, can be heavy, resulting in a cloud of insects over the water.

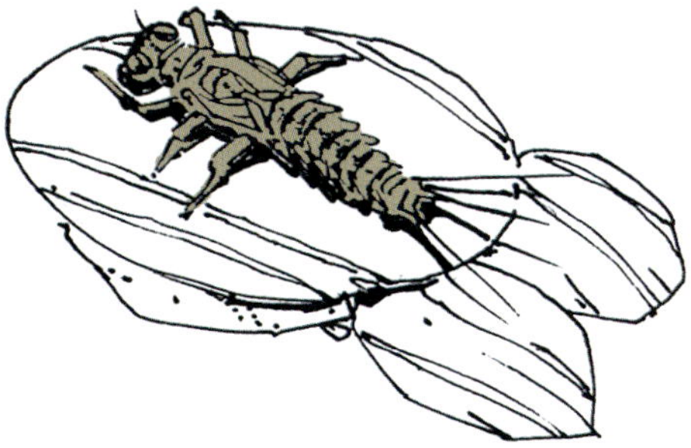

Crawler Mayfly Nymphs

Crawlers have rounded tapered bodies and are adapted to slower currents where they crawl among the vegetation feeding on river debris. Crawlers are also terrible swimmers and when washed into the current are helpless against predators. Examples of crawlers are pale morning duns and *Tricos*.

Caddis

Compared to mayflies, caddis have always maintained a lowly position in the eyes of anglers. Perhaps it's their moth-like appearance which lacks the delicate beauty of a mayfly, or maybe it's just a lack of knowledge among anglers. Caddis are without a doubt the most available insect to trout on most streams, and the more we learn about this insect the more important they are becoming.

All adult caddis have a basic form that is easy to recognize: long antennae and tent-shaped wings that fold roof-like over the body when the insect is resting. Common colors include olive, brown, cream, black, and orange. Sizes vary from very large, October caddis, to the small, sedges. Caddis larvae are a varied group most often distinguished by the types of cases they build or their behavioral patterns.

Caddis have a complete metamorphosis; that is, their development goes from egg, to larva, to pupa, and then adult. The last three stages are important to the angler.

In the larval stage, caddis are like caterpillars and live in one of three ways: building a case, living freely along the bottom without a case, or building a net with which to filter out food from the river. The easiest to identify are the case-building caddis, because one can easily find these cases on any river, clinging to rocks and logs. Free-living and net-building caddis are more difficult to find because they are hidden among the rocks in faster water.

Burrower Mayfly Nymph

Burrowers have long slender bodies and live most of their life buried in the soft substrata of river bottoms. Examples of burrowers are big yellow mayflies (*Hexagenia*), and brown drakes.

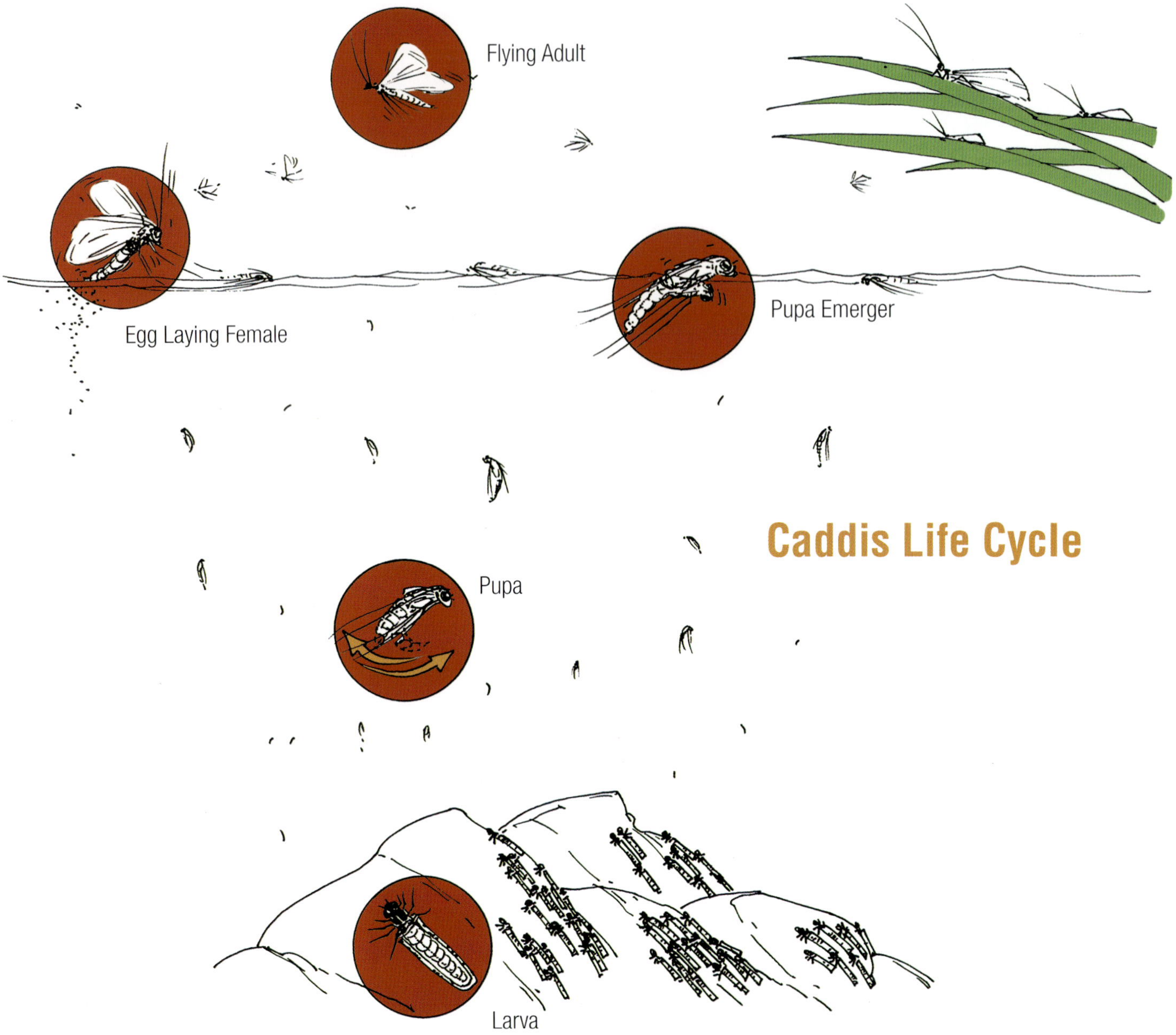

Caddis Life Cycle

Pupation, the transition between larva and adult, occurs when free-living and net-builder caddis encase themselves in a shuck and begin a maturity cycle which leads to emergence. Cased caddis also transform in their cases prior to emergence. After maturity, the pupa emerges and makes its ascent to the surface, where it hatches into an adult and flies to streamside vegetation to get ready for mating. After mating, caddis return to the river to either lay their eggs on the surface of the water or dive under the water to lay eggs on the bottom of the stream.

Most caddis are eaten by trout when they are in their larval or pupal stage during emergence. For this reason, subsurface flies are very effective in water where caddis are found. Adults are of less importance because they don't spend much time on the water, but most anglers find success fishing adult patterns such as an Elk Hair Caddis.

Beadhead Copper John and Serendipity Nymph Patterns

Non-specific patterns that work on any river.

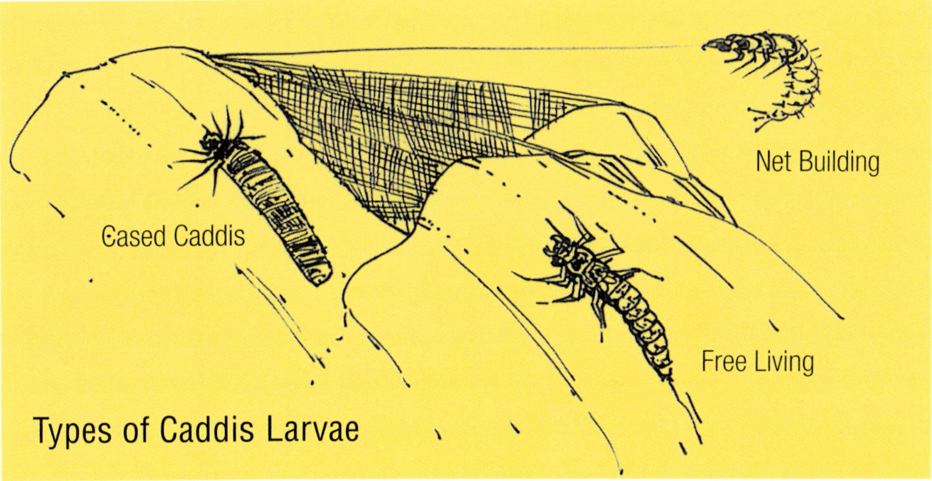

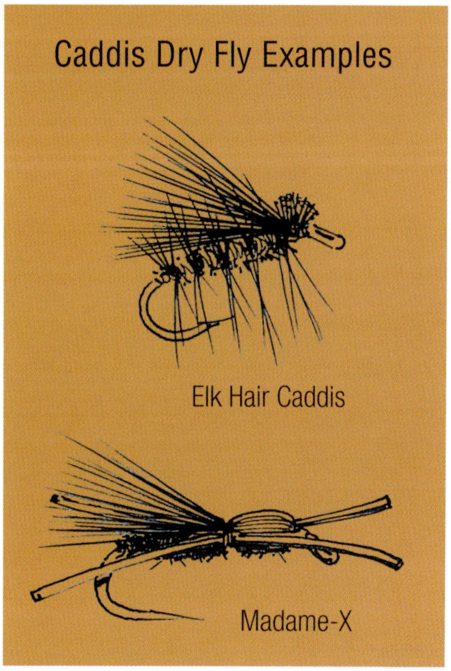

Stoneflies

Stoneflies are abundant in most North American rivers and streams and form an important part of the trout's diet. Stonefly hatches are legendary on many rivers such as the Deschutes in Oregon or the Henry's Fork in Idaho, and draw anglers from all over the world. Stoneflies come in a great variety, but the most common are the giant salmonfly, golden stonefly, and the smaller varieties of yellow Sallies and small black stoneflies.

Adult stoneflies are easy to identify, with wings that fold down flat over the body when at rest. Hatches are usually dense, with the adults covering anything on land, including anglers. Fish gobble these large insects with slashing rises.

Salmonfly hatches require large dry flies to represent these big insects.

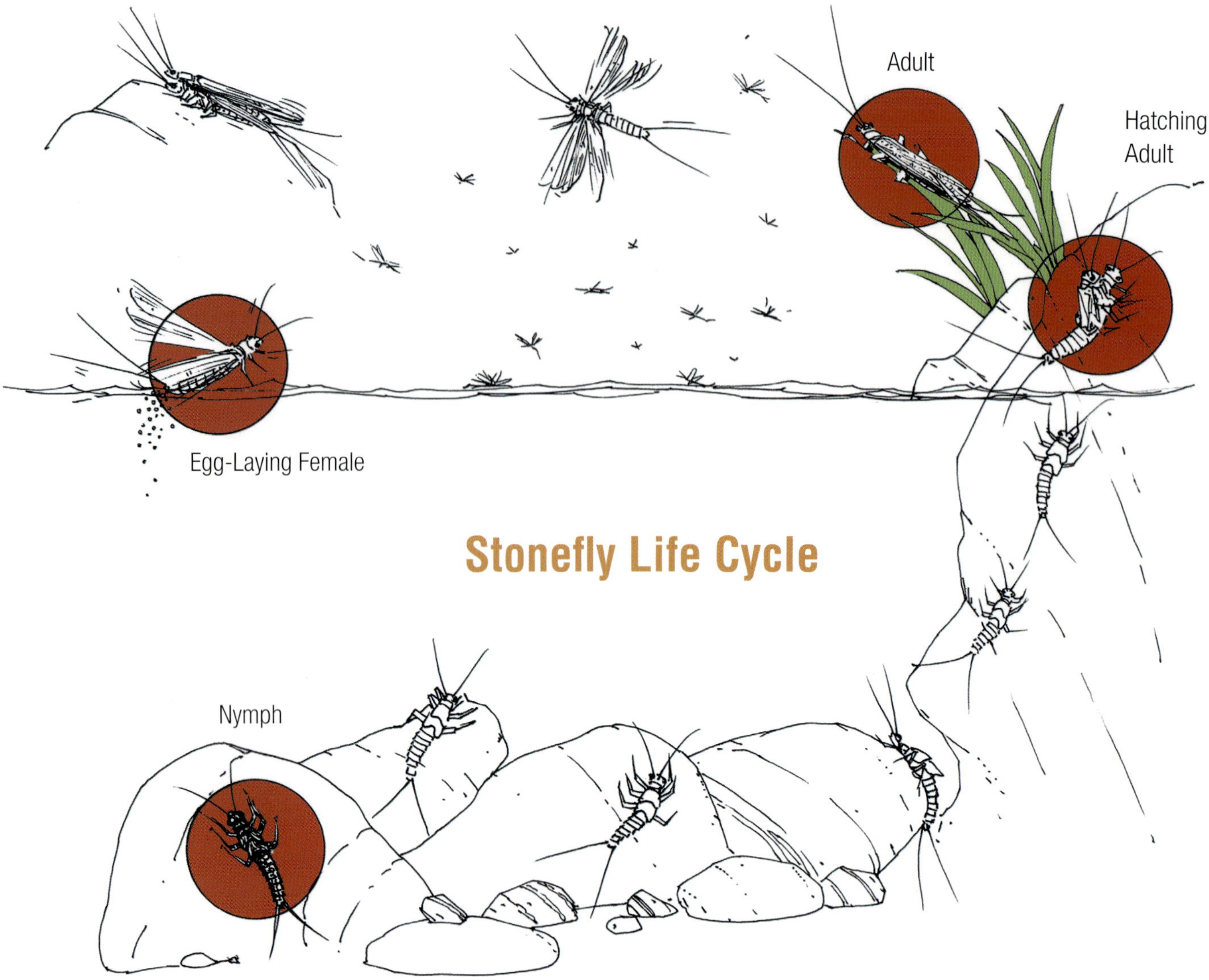

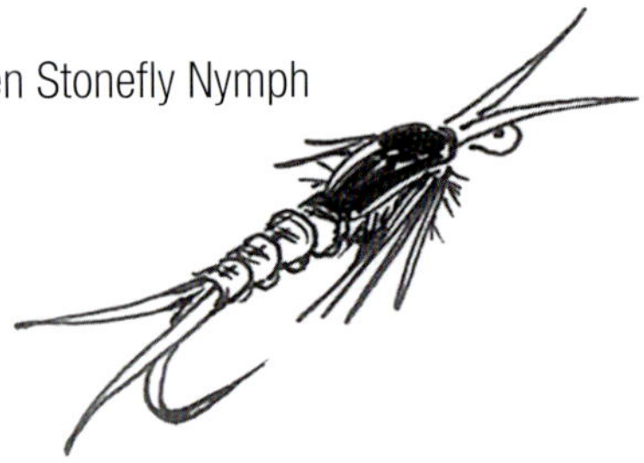

Golden Stonefly Nymph

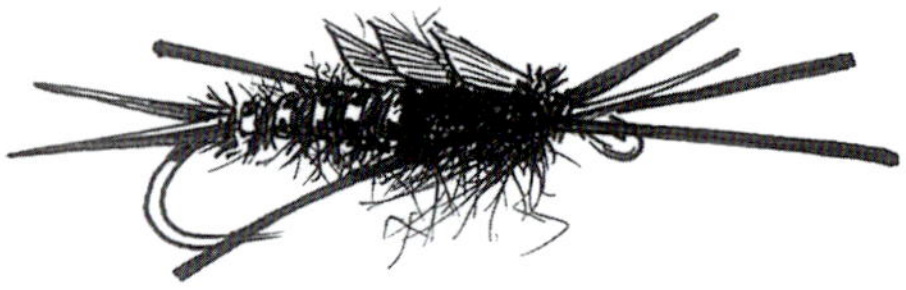

Kaufmann's Stonefly Nymph

Similar to mayflies, stoneflies have an incomplete metamorphosis: nymph and adult. Nymphs can live in their sub-aquatic state for one to three years, so they are very available to trout year-round. Nymphs are tenacious crawlers and clingers and seek the dark places on river bottoms in faster current, but they are helpless swimmers. Nymphs that break free in currents are very vulnerable to trout.

Upon emergence, the nymphs will crawl out onto land structures, such as rocks and grass, in order to emerge an adult. After mating, the females will return to the water to lay their eggs. Returning females usually generate a fish feeding frenzy when egg-laying adults wind up helpless on the water. Both dry flies and nymphs are effective for catching trout.

Terrestrials

Terrestrial insects are those that are born and live on land, but which frequently end up in the water as helpless swimmers to be fed on by trout. The most famous of these insects is the grasshopper, and many rivers are famous for producing great fishing with these patterns.

Other terrestrials include crickets, ants, flying ants, termites, beetles, bees, caterpillars, inchworms, jassids (leaf hoppers), cicada, moths and even spiders.

Primarily, these insects are available to trout during the summer months when they are active and living near the stream environment. The occurrence of terrestrials on the water is unpredictable and rarely constitutes anything like a hatch, but one can come across instances when an abundance of these insects are on the water. When an angler chooses to fish these patterns, they are doing so in the hopes that a trout is familiar with these insects and will take the opportunity to feed on them.

Angler knowledge about fishing terrestrials is on the rise. It may be said that terrestrial patterns are an underrated and undiscovered way to catch trout.

Mike Lawson, in his beautiful book *Spring Creeks*, has said, "If I had to pick one single fly to fish on spring-creek waters, without hesitation I would choose a black beetle."

The recent attention given to terrestrials by many seasoned and respected anglers such as Mike Lawson and Gary LaFontaine has a lot of anglers reevaluating the importance of terrestrial patterns in their fishing.

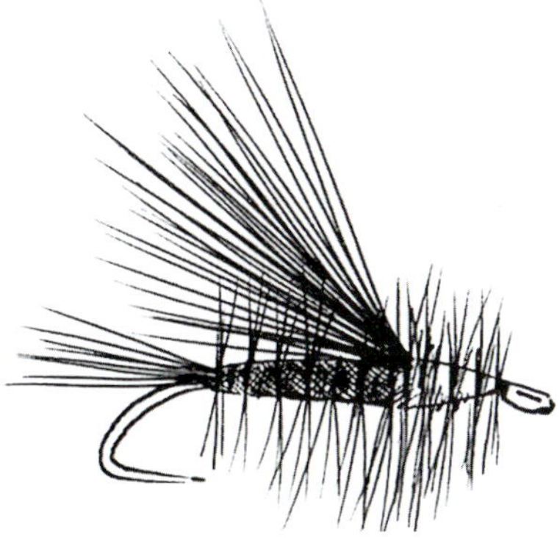

Salmonfly, Large Dry Fly

Golden Stonefly, Large Dry Fly

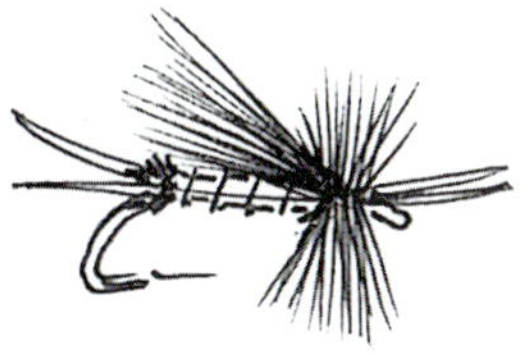

Yellow Sally Dry Fly
(aka, small golden stonefly)

Other Food Forms

This category represents a hodgepodge of food items that are frequently available to fish most of the year and on any river or stream. Most of these other food forms live their entire life in the river. Examples include freshwater crustaceans such as scuds, sowbugs and crayfish; leeches and aquatic worms; backswimmers and water boatmen; fish eggs; and the very important forage fish such as minnows and sculpin.

Terrestrial Insects

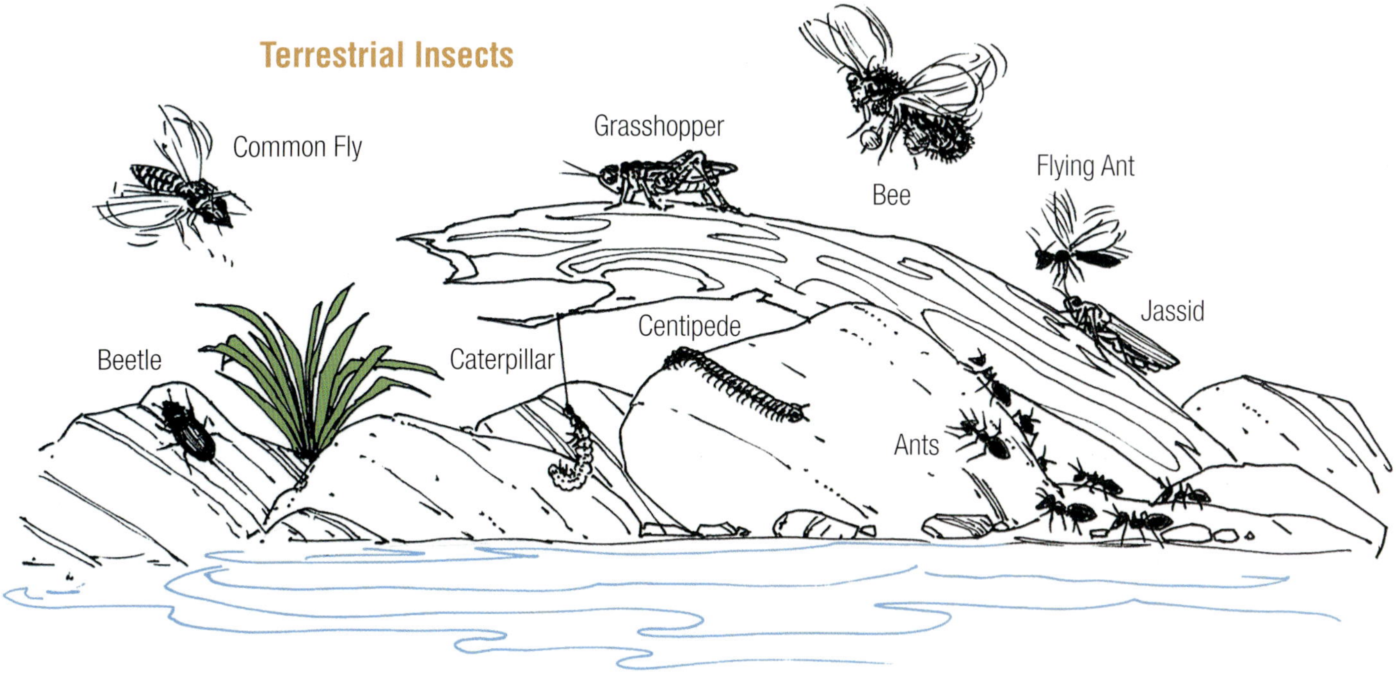

Underwater Food Forms

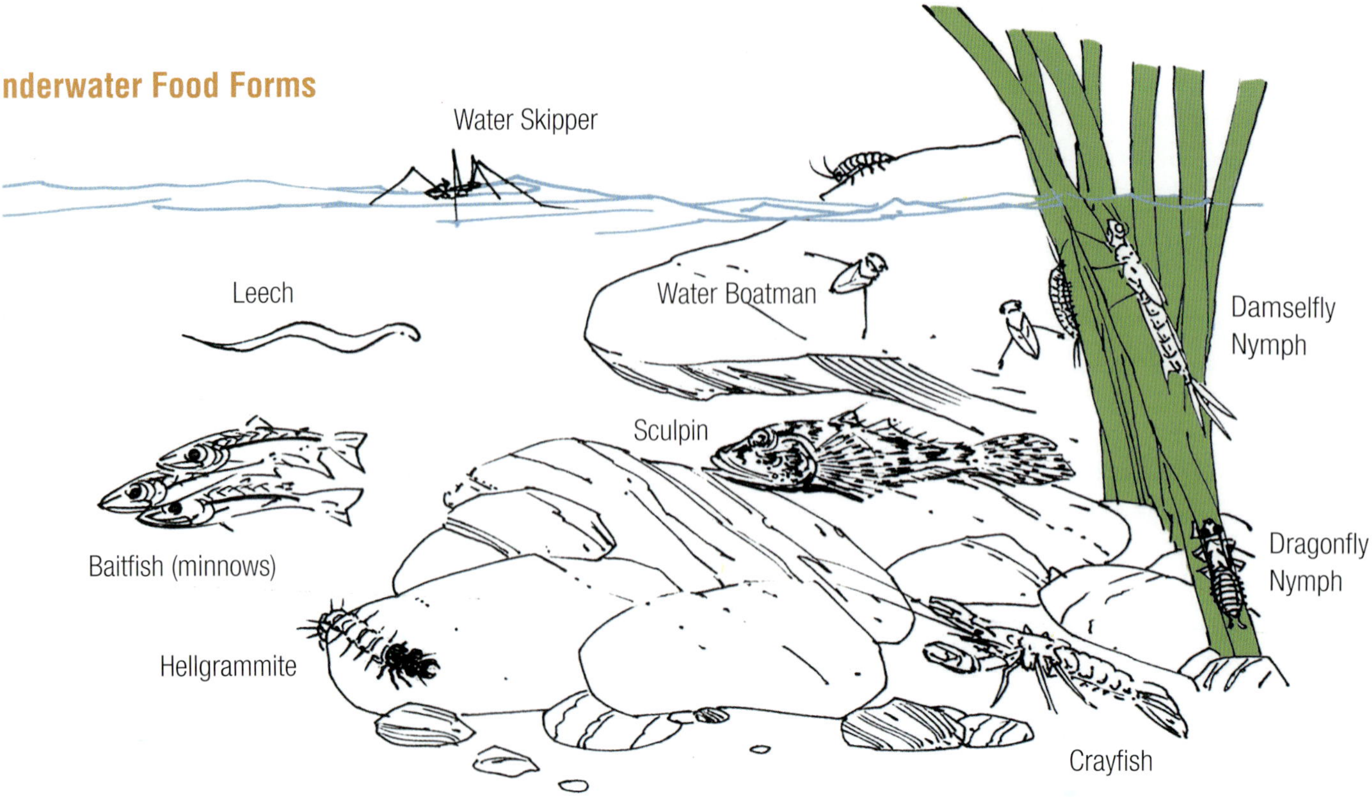

Terrestrial Fly Patterns

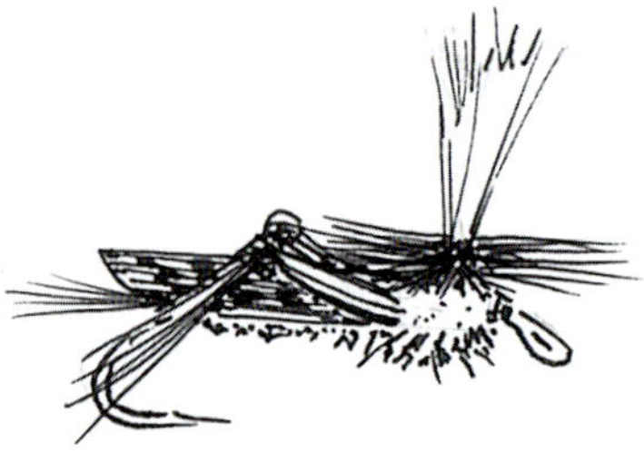

Parachute Grasshopper

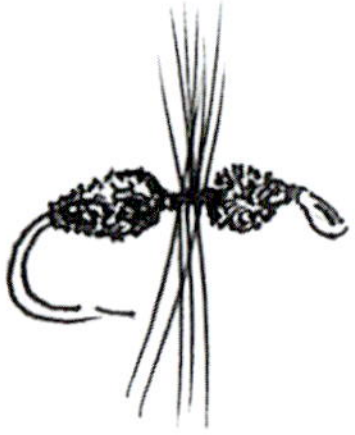

Ant

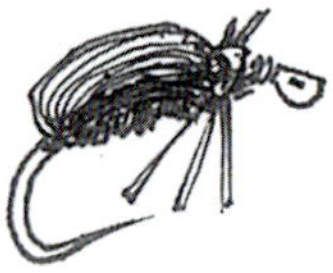

Beetle

There is a theory among anglers and biologists that larger fish sustain their size not by feeding on small insects, which they do, but on a steady diet of higher protein items such as other fish, eggs, worms, baitfish, crayfish and leeches. In fact, larger fish are frequently caught on large streamer patters or egg patterns which represent many of these items.

Grasshopper and other terrestrial patterns can produce excellent dry-fly fishing in summer.

Dry Flies

Wet Flies

Adams

Royal Wulff

Soft Hackle Hare's Ear

Elk Hair Caddis

Stimulator

Soft Hackle, Peacock

Humpy

Parachute Adams

Sparkle Caddis Pupa Olive

Swisher's Madam X

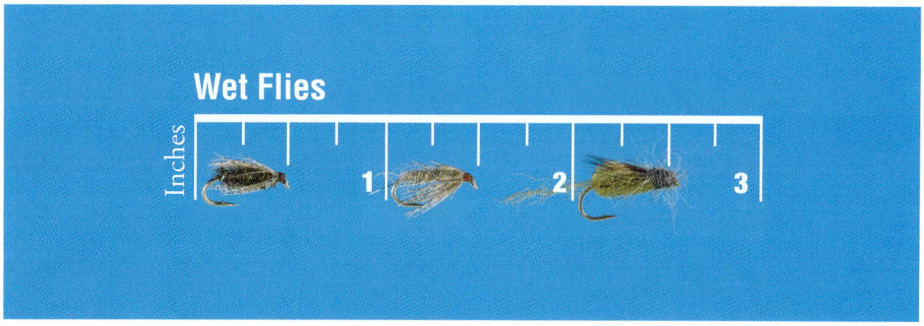

Terrestrials

Black Flying Ant

Hopper

Chubby Chernobyl

Foam Beetle

Streamers

Muddler Minnow

Woolly Bugger

Rickard's Seal Bugger

Zonker

Emergers

Flash Cripple, Gray

Juan's Ice Emerger, PMD

Brewer's Butthead Sparkle Dun

Flies Courtesy of Montana Fly Company

Streamers

Nymphs

BH Hare's Ear

BH Prince Nymph

Gold Ribbed Hare's Ear

BH Black Stonefly

Pheasant Tail

BH Flashback Pheasant Tail

Emergers

Copper Bob

Terrestrials

Nymphs

7

Rivers, Reading Water & Locating Trout

"I still don't know why I Fish or why other men Fish, except that we like it and it makes us think and feel . . . Perhaps Fishing is, for me, only an excuse to be near Rivers. If so, I'm glad I thought of it."

—Roderick Haig-Brown,
A River Never Sleeps *(1946)*

The heart of fly-angling is catching, landing, admiring and releasing a beautiful trout, but equally compelling for most anglers is the beauty found in the environments of trout rivers. In a fly-fisher's soul, these two things come together, become inseparable, and give expression to the totality of our sport. This is nowhere better expressed than in the now immortal words of author Norman Maclean when he wrote, ". . . in the arctic half-light of the canyon, all existence fades to a being with my soul and memories and the sounds of the Big Blackfoot River and a four-count rhythm and the hope that a fish will rise . . . Eventually, all things merge into one, and a river runs through it . . . I am haunted by waters."

Environmental elements are as much a part of the fishing experience as catching fish. Here we begin to understand the multi-disciplinary approach to this sport, which can include stream hydrology, entomology, meteorology, ecology, and ichthyology (study of fishes). Some of these issues, such as trout and insects, we have already discussed. In this chapter we will get a glimpse into the nature of rivers: their anatomy, how they provide for the needs of a trout, and where and how to locate trout in a river.

Dick Winter fishing the evening black drake hatch on the Upper Williamson River in Oregon.

Craig Schuhmann

Robert Schuhmann

A spring creek's subtle character often belies the challenging conditions and trout faced by anglers.

Where your fishing journey will take you is still unknown, and that is why it's good to begin where you are, by fishing the rivers around you. I encourage you to use the information from this chapter and start exploring your "home waters," rivers which are conveniently located and do not require a lot of travel time or preparation. On your home waters you can hone your craft and learn to identify certain types of rivers and the ways in which they support trout populations. Armed with this knowledge, you will be able to approach any river in a respectful and productive manner.

Here we begin to understand the multi-disciplinary approach to this sport, which can include stream hydrology, entomology, meteorology, ecology, and ichthyology (study of fishes).

Types of Rivers

There are three types of rivers: freestones, spring creeks and tailwaters. Each is a unique river environment with variables such as water quality, stream flows, and insect populations that support trout in different ways.

Freestone rivers have high-gradient flows, meaning they begin in higher elevations and have an unimpeded flow of water from source to mouth. Typically, one thinks of a mountain stream, tumbling and

Craig Schuhmann

River banks such as these often indicate deeply undercut banks and protection for wary trout.

falling down mountainsides through boulders, rocks, canyons and forests, but freestone rivers can be large, medium or small. Water sources include any combination of glacier melt, lakes, mountain runoff and underground springs. Thus, freestone river environments are volatile, with high waters in spring and low waters in summer and fall. Many freestone rivers are ephemeral, meaning they can dry up during the summer months when no run-off is present.

Trout in most freestone rivers favor the cool headwaters, leaving lower sections of river to warmwater species such as bass and panfish.

Trout in most freestone rivers favor the cool headwaters, leaving lower sections of river to warmwater species such as bass and panfish. Fluctuating water temperatures and levels make life for trout and insects unpredictable. Although not always the case, the volatility of freestone rivers means smaller fish and sparse food supply, making trout in these rivers easier to catch. The best fishing on freestone rivers occurs when water levels are cool and stabilized, such as in late spring or early summer after a mountain runoff.

Spring creeks are rivers that have their source at an underground spring; because of this constant source, spring creeks are extremely stable, with very little fluctuation in water flows and temperatures. Their nutrient-rich waters create healthy, big trout and abundant insect populations. Spring creeks are generally unaffected by seasonal changes such as droughts, spring runoff, and summer high temperatures; therefore, fishing remains good throughout the seasons. Some common characteristics of spring creeks are cold, crystal-clear water, slow currents, and aquatic weed growth. Some famous spring creeks include Silver Creek in Idaho and Armstrong Creek in Montana.

Spring creeks often represent the high benchmark for fly-anglers in terms of difficulty and selective trout. There are two reasons for this: fishing regulations and fish selectivity. Most spring creeks have catch-and-release fishing regulations, and fish will become more wary and selective after being caught multiple times in a year. Selectivity is also a factor because trout have all their needs met in a spring creek and have little need to move around to different sections of the river. Due to abundant insect populations and clear waters, imitations are carefully inspected. Spring creeks generally require smaller tippets, more representational flies (even exact imitations), and rods and lines that deliver delicate presentations.

Tailwater, or tailrace, rivers are trout rivers that begin downstream from a dam. Some of the more famous tailwater fisheries are the Green River in Utah, Deschutes in Oregon, and the Henry's Fork of the Snake River in Idaho. Tailwater fisheries appear as normal rivers, but their environment is artificially managed with the release of water from dams.

Many tailwaters mimic the characteristics of a freestone river with faster, boulder-strewn water flowing through deep gorges. Other tailwaters have a spring-creek appearance with gentle currents and abundant weed growth but are generally much larger rivers. Either way, tailwater fisheries share many attributes associated with spring creeks: nutrient-rich waters, constant temperatures, abundant insect populations and large trout. One drawback to tailwaters is the seasonal or daily fluctuations in water levels, which can stress fish and suppress insect hatches. Also, tailwaters can be greatly affected by upstream water quality coming from the use of water behind the dams.

Tailwater fisheries can be very demanding, and an angler's skill and fly selection is important. The same conditions that create selective and wary trout in spring creeks also apply to tailwater rivers; because trout in tailwaters have most of their needs met in one location, their movement is limited and they can be comfortable and happy in one location their whole life.

Tailwater fisheries share many attributes associated with spring creeks: nutrient-rich waters, constant temperatures, abundant insect populations and large trout.

Craig Schuhmann

Underwater obstructions such as logs and rocks make great trout habitat.

Needs of a Trout in a River

Regardless of which type of river you are fishing, trout always have the same needs: food, cover (protection from predators), and comfort (water temperature, oxygenation, current speed). The best places to find trout in a river are in areas where all three of these criteria are met at one time. Fish will sacrifice one or two of these needs for a short period of time if there is a payoff. For example, a fish may feed in an open flat, sacrificing cover and comfort if food is abundant, but only while the food is available. Likewise, fish will sacrifice comfort to feed in the fast current of a riffle, while maintaining cover and food, but when the food is gone, they will return to more comfortable currents in runs and pools.

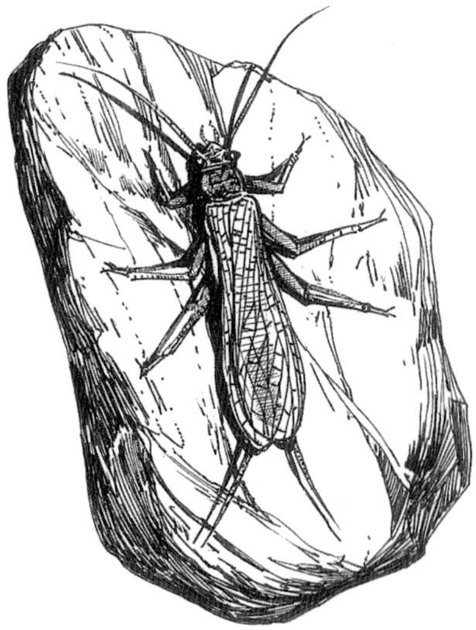

Stonefly

Feeding lanes are generally places where river currents come together, such as around rocks or other obstructions, and concentrate drifting insects into a small area.

Food

Trout feed according to a basic formula: the energy obtained from an item of food must be greater than the energy they expend to receive it. Trout position themselves in a river to intercept food; these are called feeding lanes. Feeding lanes are generally places where river currents come together, such as around rocks or other obstructions, and concentrate drifting insects into a small area. The most active feeding periods of trout are connected to periods of the greatest insect activity. In warmer months, insects are active in the early and late hours of the day. In colder months, insects are active during the most comfortable parts of the day, typically in the afternoon.

Trout feed both selectively and opportunistically. Selective feeding occurs when the trout key in on one particular insect form at the exclusion of all others; usually this is the most abundant food form. Selectivity can also be the result of catch-and-release fishing regulations, such that a fish will become more wary of imitations as they are caught by anglers more than once. Opportunistic feeding occurs most of the time, but particularly when trout are looking for food and/or food is scarce. Many anglers theorize that trout feed opportunistically most of the time and this is why attractor flies work so well.

Cover

Trout are survivalists, and when they are not concerned with food they seek protection from currents and safety from predators. Types of cover include rocks, choppy water, logs, undercut banks, overhanging brush or trees, weed beds, shadows, and deep water. Provided there are adequate water temperatures and flows, trout will hold in these places a good portion of any day. Areas of cover may also be places where food is concentrated by river currents.

Comfort

Comfort for a trout means water temperatures and oxygen content. These factors are directly related to a fish's ability to compete for food, develop and grow, and spawn. Optimum water temperatures for most trout are between 58 and 68 degrees. Higher water temperatures between 70 and 80 degrees cause inactivity, lethargy and ultimately death. Lower temperatures between 50 and 40 degrees are ideal for spawning, but temperatures below 32 can cause death. Fish love aerated water, one factor that helps deliver an adequate supply of oxygen to the fish.

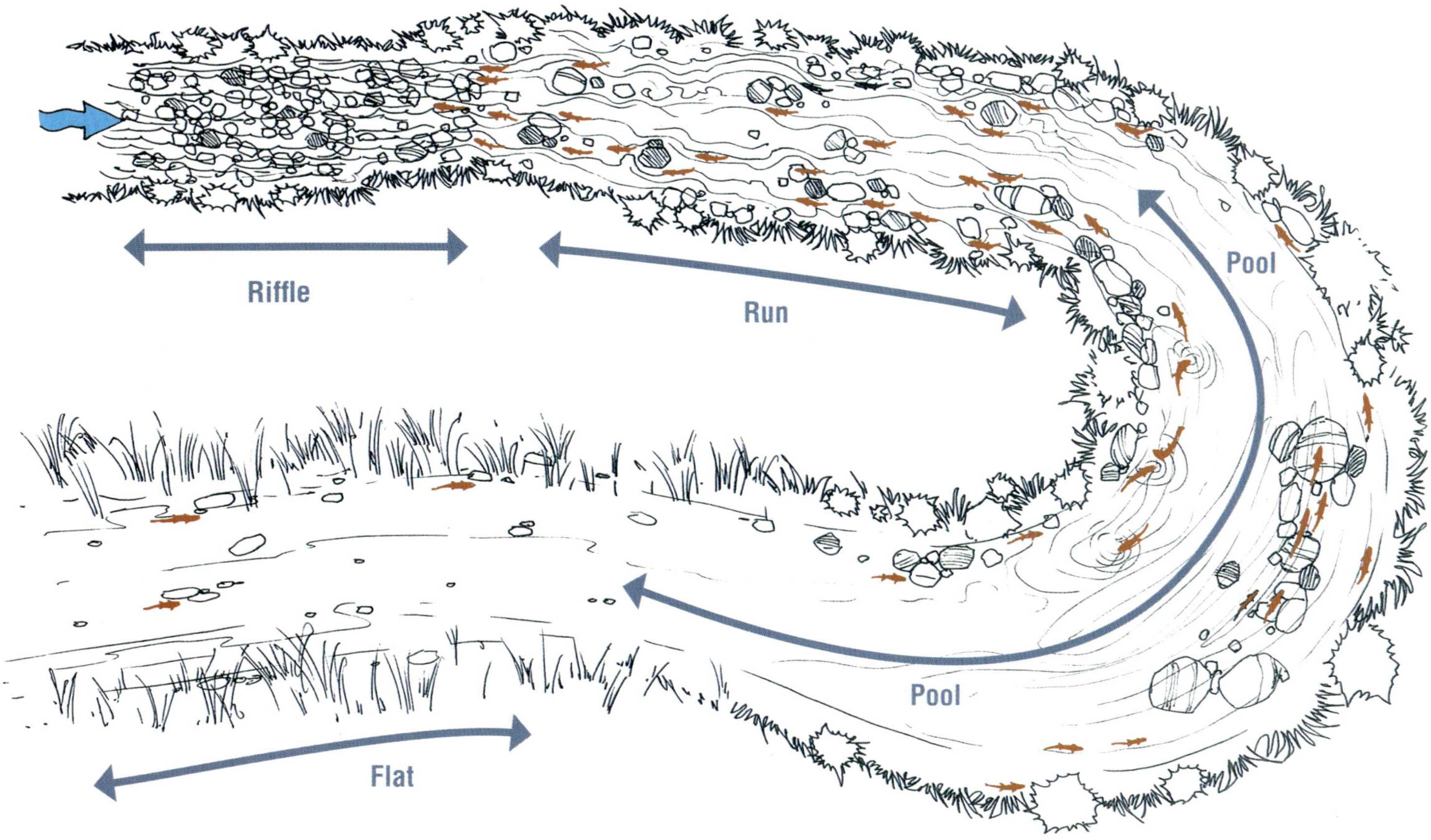

Anatomy of a River and Reading Water

Knowing the anatomy of a river, as well as the needs of a fish, will tell you where to find trout. "Reading water" is the phrase given to an angler's ability to discern the parts of a river and determine where trout may be holding. Trout will move in and out of the different parts of a river depending on their needs.

All beginning anglers struggle with the art of reading water. This is a learned skill that takes patience and perceptive abilities. Deciphering the parts of a river means recognizing visual clues to what the water is doing as well as knowing what lies beneath the water, and this can only be gained by experience. To help you understand how to read water I will discuss each part of a river by answering the following three questions. Whenever you're unsure about what part of a river you're looking at, just ask yourself:

1. What is the speed of the water?
2. What is the surface doing?
3. What is the water's depth?

Riffles

Shallow, faster water of one to three feet deep. The river bottom in a riffle is composed of cobbles or rocks which create the broken water surface. Riffles are the shallowest part of a river and the best producer of aquatic insects such as mayflies, stoneflies and caddis.

Riffle, Run, Pool, Flat

Fish will move around in a river depending on their needs.

Understanding the parts of a river and how to identify them will aid you in your ability to find fish and determine which flies to use.

"Reading water" is the phrase given to an angler's ability to discern the parts of a river and determine where trout may be holding.

Riffles are the best place to begin fishing a river because this is where a majority of insects live. They are also the easiest places to catch fish because trout are less spooky with the broken water surface, less selective, and have to make quick decisions about their food. Fish will feed in a riffle and feel protected from predators, but it is not good holding water and trout will move to more restful water when food disappears.

Fish hold in riffles, seeking places that offer food and protection from currents, such as behind rocks or logs and in current seams where fast and slow water meet.

This beautiful river in Montana is a great example of pocket water and riffles; often the most productive areas of any river.

Craig Schuhmann

Runs often hold big trout and require weighted flies or lines to get flies deep.

Runs

Runs usually begin where riffles end. Runs are deeper than riffles, three to six feet deep, and have boiled rather than choppy water due to larger rocks and boulders. The current can be either fast or slow, but is generally slower than riffles. Slower, deeper water means fish can find more places that meet their requirements for food, comfort and cover. Fish often move into runs after they have fed in a riffle.

Insect populations in runs are not as abundant as riffles and are often fed by the riffles above. Fish holding in runs can be harder to catch because they may be less interested in eating and they have more time to inspect food, therefore presentations need to be more imitative of the actual food forms. Fishing runs can require more specialized gear such as sink-tip lines.

The best holding lies in a run are at the head of the run where it meets a riffle or pool; behind rocks, boulders, ledges, and logs; in current seams; and along the banks.

The best holding lies in a run are at the head of the run where it meets a riffle or pool; behind rocks, boulders, ledges, and logs; in current seams; and along the banks.

Finding success in a pool requires techniques that are similar to stillwater fishing; retrieve styles and patience are your best tools.

These four areas of a river—riffle, run, pool and flat—are the macro levels to a river.

Pools

The deepest and slowest part of a river, smooth on the surface. This is where fish come to rest and hide. There are three parts to a pool: the head, body and tailout. The head feeds the pool from the run or riffle; the body is usually deep, slow, almost still water; the tailout is where the water shelves, becoming shallower and faster, and is the transition point into a run or riffle.

Pools often hold the largest fish in the river because all the criteria of comfort, cover and food are met in abundance. Fewer aquatic insects live in pools, but food forms there are bigger, such as crayfish, minnows, sculpin, leeches and trout fry. Certain aquatic insects, particularly the swimmers, live in pools, which can create good dry-fly fishing. Fishing pools is the most difficult area to catch fish in a river because fish have lots of time to inspect their food, so anglers need specialized techniques and equipment.

The best holding lies in a pool are at the head, where the water becomes deeper and transitions from the riffle or run; along the banks in well-protected areas such as undercut banks, overhanging brush or trees, or downed logs; around submerged boulders; and in the tailouts.

Flats

Flats are created when the river bottom is smooth, and the depth of the water is one to four feet deep. Flats have an even flow and a smooth surface. They can be fast or slow. Weed beds are common in flats and offer a concentration of food such as midges, scuds and mayflies. There can be very little cover in a flat, so trout are often compromising security in exchange for food.

Fishing flats can be demanding with slow currents and shallow, clear water. Anglers are easily visible to the fish, which are also wary of predators. Some of the best dry-fly fishing occurs in flats, and they are the place to go when hatches are occurring. Small flies, fine tippet, and delicate presentations are often needed.

Fish can hold anywhere in a flat, but the choice places are around weed beds, along banks with cover, and around any obstacles such as rocks or depressions in the river bed.

These four areas of a river—riffle, run, pool and flat—are the macro levels to a river. But there is also a micro level to reading water. That is, identifying areas in the river that are breaks from current and offer protection or feeding lanes. Some of these we have already discussed, such as behind rocks, around sunken trees, in the shadows of streamside vegetation, beneath undercut banks, and in current seams. These features can be found in all parts of the river.

Other areas to look for are back eddies, slack water along banks, pockets in the corners of riffles, under spilling water such as waterfalls. When reading water, learn to look for and identify variations in the current; these will be clues to what lies beneath the water, and they are always possible holding places for fish. Experience and perceptive observations are going to be your best tools.

Other areas to look for are back eddies, slack water along banks, pockets in the corners of riffles, under spilling water such as waterfalls.

Fishing a shallow flat, requires stealth, but can produce some of the best dry-fly fishing during a hatch.

"Fishing takes anglers to the best places, at the best times of year."
~Anonymous~

Stalking

Locating trout, sometimes called stalking, is an art practiced by few and overlooked by many. The reason it's overlooked is that it takes time away from fishing and most anglers lack the patience to sit and watch the river for clues to where trout may be hiding. Another reason anglers don't stalk is because they don't believe they will see any fish; better, they figure, to get in the river and "chuck and chance it". In most cases anglers will fair far better and catch more trout if they take time to slow down and look for clues to what the fish may be doing. One common suggestion made by experienced anglers is to approach a river without having strung-up your rod. Not having a fly on the end of your line is a great way to slow yourself down so you'll take time to observe what is happening around you.

The following are a few suggestions which, even practiced in part, will lead to more success than if they were not followed at all. I will cover briefly how to approach a trout stream, methods for spotting trout, probable places to look for trout and rise forms.

In most cases anglers will fair far better and catch more trout if they take time to slow down and look for clues to what the fish may be doing.

The Approach

Clothing

Match your clothing to whatever background you're fishing against. When fishing against woodlands wear browns, greens, dark blues or similar dark clothing. When there is little bank cover and you're fishing against the sky, wear light greens, blues and yellows.

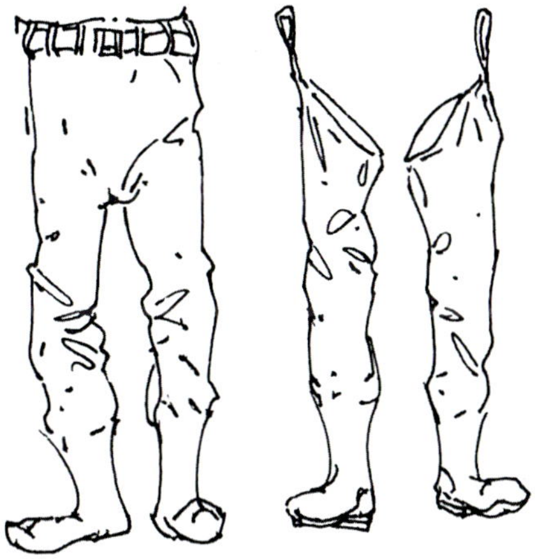

Wading pants and hip waders are nice alternatives to chest waders during the summer months or when fishing shallow water.

Movement

Mitigate movement when you think you're in the vicinity of fish. This includes not only your body but also your rod, both of which should be slung low. Walk in a crouch. Avoid too much head movement and remove all shiny objects such as jewelry and watches. Eyeglasses can cast a glare, so use matted films over your lenses or polarizing sunglasses that are not mirrored.

On the Bank

Avoid walking over undercut banks, sloshing through marsh lands, jumping on logs that may be extended into the water, crashing through bankside bushes or rattling stones in a dry rocky patch. Avoid casting a shadow when the sun is behind you.

In the Water

If you do need to get in the water, approach the water's edge and potential lies carefully. Take note of anything that may make a disturbance as you enter the water, such as rattling over stones, stirring up mud, and moving through aquatic grasses or marsh. Note any obstacles that will need to be avoided, rocks, downed trees, or islands that have to be climbed over. Obstacles can also be your friend, blocking water disturbances and giving you a closer vantage point under cover.

Cover

The best cover is to keep back from the bank as far as possible while still being able to see the water you want to fish. If the bank is brush-lined, use the tree trunk and foliage as cover to peer beyond into the water. Keep low when there is no brush and walk carefully.

The best cover is to keep back from the bank as far as possible while still being able to see the water you want to fish.

Wading

One cannot enter the water without making a disturbance. This is why most angling writers suggest wading only if it is necessary. Wading, when necessary, is almost always to get closer to the fish, not to scout the water.

Wading can help you move up from behind a fish or approach from a lower angle. Steps in the water should be deliberate to mitigate noise and prevent wakes, scraping against rocks, moving rocks or kicking up debris (especially if you're wading to approach a downstream fish). Wading upstream, even in the shallowest water, will invariably create a bow-wave and send ripples far ahead of you.

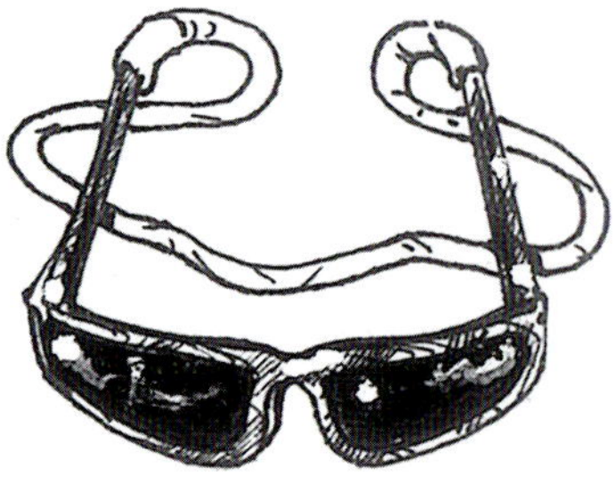

How to See Trout

The Eyes

Limit the amount of light entering your eyes by wearing a brimmed or long-billed hat to shade your eyes from the sun. Use polarizing sunglasses, the best you can afford. Glass is the best. A more expensive option is Photochromatic lenses which are tinted to get lighter in the shadows and darker in the sun. Plastic and polycarbonate lenses scratch more easily. Different shades of lenses cut glare differently: amber is a good all-around color.

Using the Light

The best conditions for seeing in the water are sunny, windless days when the sun is overhead or behind you. The worst conditions are windy days, gray days, or when the sun is facing you. When this happens, you can do a few things to help: obtain a higher perspective such as a hill or tree; use the shadows from foliage on the far bank to cut glare and get a view into the water; isolate a single shadow that cuts the glare and scan that area as best you can.

Concentration and Confidence

Focus on the river's bottom, not the surface. In order to do this you may have to stand still or move very slowly. If the water looks like a

probable holding area, mentally resolve that the fish are in the water. It's easier to see something you think is there.

What to Look For

Do not expect to see a whole fish. You may only see parts of a fish or movement. The tail is often the first thing you will see when looking for fish because it's in constant movement. Things to look for are wiggling or darting movements, fish shadows, the whites of a feeding fish's mouth, and the flash of their sides as they move.

Where Trout Lie

Probable places to look for trout are under bridges, around dams, overhanging trees and brush, undercut banks, behind rocks and obstacles, in weed beds, pockets and channels, around foam and debris lines, riffles, and in pools.

Probable places to look for trout are under bridges, around dams, overhanging trees and brush, undercut banks, behind rocks...

Clues to Feeding Behavior

Rise Forms

Rise forms are a much discussed and debated topic among anglers, but the key insight of all this discussion is that there are many different rise forms, and each is an indication of various feeding habits and food preferences. For this reason alone, it's important to take notice of some of these different rise forms on your local rivers.

Sip or Kiss Rise

Indicates the trout is feeding on a surface insect, such as a drifting mayfly or caddis. The sip is an easy, slow rise, often repetitive, in which the trout will expose his head or mouth above the water. Anglers will often hear an audible kissing noise or sucking sound. This fish will most likely accept a well-presented dry fly.

Sipping Rise

Head and Tail Rise

Often mistaken for a sip or kiss rise because the top of the head, back and tail are visible to the angler. The head and tail rise is an indicator that the fish is eating just below the surface on emergers or other subsurface insects. Think of a fish skimming the water surface for something that lies just beneath the surface. This fish may completely ignore a dry fly in preference for an emerger or floating nymph.

Head and Tail Rise

Tailing Trout

Not a frequent sight except on certain types of trout streams, such as spring creeks. Here the trout's tail is the only thing exposed. This rise form usually occurs where trout are feeding on the bottom and the trout is nose down, rooting through aquatic grasses for insects. I have only seen this rise form on slow-moving spring creeks that have dense aquatic grasses loaded with scuds and snails. This fish is looking for nymphs and other bottom- or grass-dwelling insects.

The Slash

This is the most violent of rise forms, loud and splashy. Slash rise forms are a great indicator that the fish may be feeding on terrestrial insects or minnows. These are sporadic rise forms, rarely occurring with any discernable succession. This fish may accept a well-presented grasshopper or beetle pattern, as well as a fast-swinging streamer.

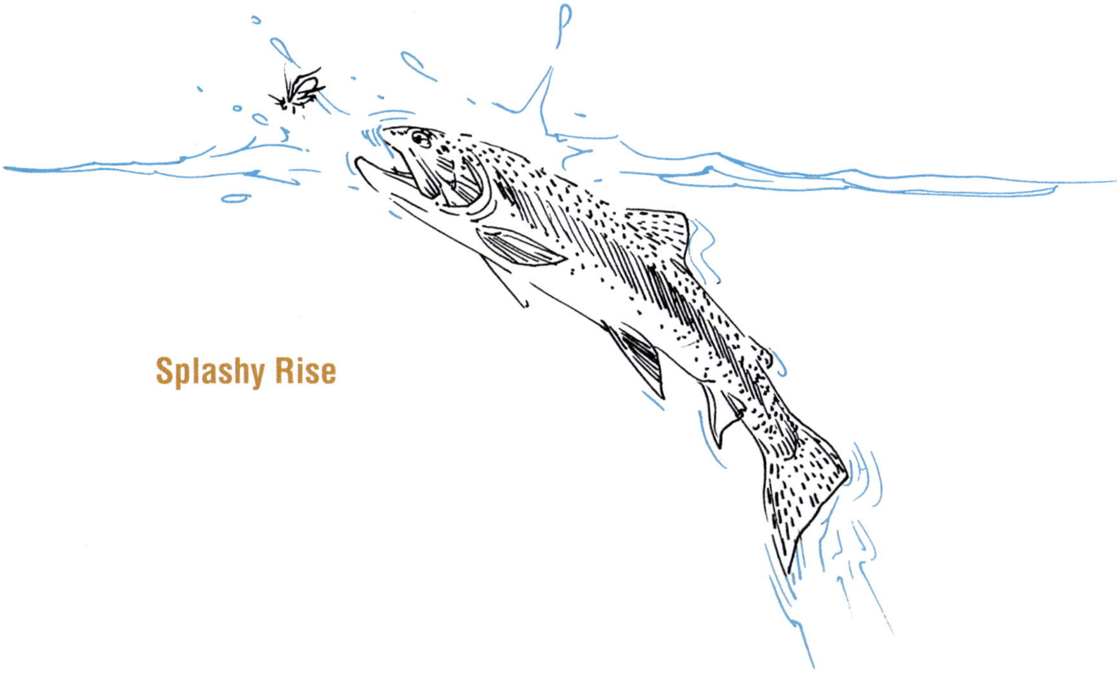

The Boil or Subsurface Rise

These happen under the surface with only a slight upsurge of water showing on the surface. Boils are created by the displacement of water under the surface. Due to their subtlety, these are the hardest rise forms to determine. Because the trout is feeding underneath the surface, a well-presented nymph, wet fly or streamer will be the best option.

Boil Rise

This fish was feeding on mayfly emergers just under the surface and succumbed to a small soft hackle swung on a floating line.

8

Presentation

Everything you have read in this book up to this point has been preparing you for the presentation. Presentation is the act of fishing, but it's so much more. It takes into account the entire process, everything you have been learning about trout: tackle selection, casting, and insects; fly selection, reading water, and spotting fish.

Two definitions of presentation have helped me in my own fishing. The first comes from Rick Hafele, a respected entomologist and angling writer, and the second from Denny Rickards, an internationally known stillwater angler. Hafele defines presentation as "getting the fly to the fish in a way trout expect to see it." Simple enough, right? It is well known that fish feed in zones, that is, positions in the water column where food is most available. Depending on where the food is, these zones may be on the bottom, on the surface, just under the surface or even mid-current. Here, we have to think like fish, understand what the insects are doing, and understand the limits of our tackle in presenting the fly.

Rickards' definition, though he is writing about lake fishing, still applies to rivers. He defines presentation as "your ability to make the fly look and act like a natural food source." For Denny, presentation involves three things: tackle selection, casting ability, and retrieve styles. Denny goes on to say, "The key to effective presentation is choosing the right tackle and techniques for the situations and conditions present. This means having balanced tackle that will deliver your fly to the fish, retrieving in a way that simulates the natural insect, and with a line that will suspend your fly for an extended period at the depth fish are feeding." In other words, getting your fly into the right zones.

In this chapter, we are going use the above definitions and define presentation to mean everything that happens from our initial cast to finishing the drift, taking into account the position of the fish, what tackle is being used, and how our fly should behave in the water.

Presentation has three components: the set-up, fishing the fly, and the finish. We will discuss each of these below and then discuss specific fishing methods.

"To be successful in fly fishing requires preparing, understanding, planning, and executing a plan, but ultimately fly fishing is still a game of chance."

***—Mike Lawson from the book* Spring Creeks**

Rick Hafele defines presentation as "getting the fly to the fish in a way trout expect to see it."

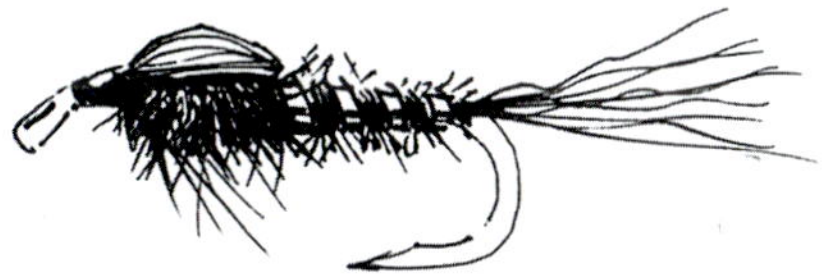

The key to effective presentation is choosing the right tackle and techniques for the situations and conditions present.

The Set-Up

Before making the first cast, identify where a fish may be holding (suspected lie), decide on an approach based on available insects or fish behavior, and think about how your line choice, tackle set-up

As a general rule, fly selection is not near as important as presentation. However, when fly selection does become important it's good to have a variety of choices.

In almost all instances, you should never cast directly at a fish. Casting directly at a fish will only spook it and ruin your chances.

and cast will make the fly look and behave in the water. Sometimes fish will tell you where they are holding and how they are feeding because we can see them in the water or we see a rise form. At other times we will not see the fish, but suspect strongly they are holding in a certain spot based on experience or because the area looks "fishy." In either case, identify a potential fish lie, even if it is an educated guess, and plan your presentation around that spot.

Learning to envision where the fish is holding relative to the position of your fly is critical for successful angling. Casting about blindly in the hopes of hitting a fish is unproductive, and if the fish does hit the fly there will be no telling why, and we would have to chalk it up to luck. Instead, fish intentionally. Develop a deep knowledge of rivers, tackle, fish, insects, and flies, to catch fish in an instructive way. Intentionality and powers of observation, not luck, is one of the fishing traits of all great anglers.

Once the fish lie, real or imagined, is identified, it's time to plan the approach. In almost all instances, you should never cast directly at a fish. Casting directly at a fish will only spook it and ruin your chances. In *The Trout and the Fly*, Clarke and Goddard made the claim that trout have great vision and, depending upon their depth in the water, can see objects as far as several feet or more in front, overhead, and off to the sides. This is called the fish's window. If you know where the fish is holding, plan to introduce the fly so that it comes into the fish's window by casting at least five feet in front of the fish. This will allow the fish sufficient time to notice your offering and decide whether to eat it. Sometimes you will see the fish pursue your fly and then at the last minute, reject it. At other times the fish ignore your fly altogether. These are two of the most frustrating and puzzling experiences in fly-fishing. Why did the fish reject the fly? Why was it ignored? Was it our presentation, the fly, or did it catch a glimpse of us? Maybe the fish is not eating? The answer could be none or all of these things, but something prevented the fish from taking the fly.

While these experiences are frustrating, they also tell us something about what the fish prefers. At this point, it is advisable to stop and reconsider your approach. One option is to change some component of our system, such as fly line, fly, or position in relation to the fish. Perhaps we need to move to different water and come back later when the fish is more interested in feeding.

If you know where the fish is holding, plan to introduce the fly so that it comes into the fish's window by casting at least five feet in front of the fish.

A Mayfly Cripple pattern has proven to be very effective, especially on selective fish.

Fishing the Fly

Once we know where the fish is holding and have an approach, it's time to fish. With the initial cast we are setting up the fly so it will drift to the fish. We are not fishing at this point, because we are assuming the fly has not yet reached the fish. Sometimes we will be surprised by getting an immediate strike after our fly hits the water, and this too will tell you something; perhaps we missed a fish lie. If you are so lucky to hit a fish this way, stop and reevaluate. Why was that fish there? What made it a good holding spot? Sometimes it pays to even walk over to that spot and examine the area to see why the fish was there.

As the fly gets closer to the suspected lie, we can assume to be fishing, because we know the fish is looking at the fly and evaluating it as potential food. What can we do here to improve our chances? Assuming we have the right fly, fly line, leader, and drift, it comes down to fly behavior, and fly behavior is determined by drag. With some exceptions that will be discussed below, drag is the enemy of all anglers. Drag is defined as the pulling action on the fly by the fly line and leader. Drag is mitigated by two things, mending and proper position of the rod tip, both of which will be discussed below in our discussion of techniques. The opposite of drag is dead drift where the fly is allowed to drift in the water at the current speed.

There are five basic fishing techniques, all related to the type of fly being used: nymphing, dry fly, emerger, wet fly, and streamers.

The Finish

When our fly reaches the fish it will either accept it, reject it, or ignore it. If the fly is not accepted then we need to finish our presentation. In almost all instances, let the fly pass by the suspected fish lie and drift well downstream out of the fish's window before picking it up and casting again. Pulling out a fly too soon may alert or spook the fish to your presence, ruining your chances at another attempt. Sometimes you will get a fish strike while your fly is moving below the targeted fish. Never overlook these moments of truth, because inadvertently hitting a fish tells us something about what fish prefer in a presentation and where they may be holding.

Picking up the fly and recasting also takes some consideration. Whenever you pick up your fly line you also pick up a lot of water, which clings to your line, leader and fly. If a cast is made back to the same spot without this consideration we may spray water all over the surface, including where the fish is holding. Spraying water on the surface will spook the fish. Pick up your line gently, make a false cast in a different direction to strip any water off the line and then cast to your presentation spot for the next drift.

There are five basic fishing techniques, all related to the type of fly being used: nymphing, dry fly, emerger, wet fly, and streamers. We will discuss each of these techniques as they pertain to fishing various parts of a river, give suggestions for riggings, and also talk about some variations related to casting and mending.

Nymphs make up 90% of the diet of trout, fishing with nymphs is a great way to catch trout and a wonderful way to explore new water that may be unfamiliar to you.

Nymph Fishing

All nymphs live on the bottom of rivers, among the rocks, gravel, debris, and in the substrate. As we learned in the previous chapter, the majority of aquatic insects live their lives in riffles and this is the first place to look for fish on any river. Also, because nymphs make up 90% of the diet of trout, fishing with nymphs is great way to catch trout and a wonderful way to explore new water that may be unfamiliar to you. Nymphs become available to trout when they break free in the current and drift helplessly just above the river bottom, or when they start their emergence to the surface to hatch into adults. Knowing how trout expect to see nymphs in a riffle will help you in your presentation techniques.

Nymphs are fished with weight, added to the fly during the tying process or to the leader in the form of split shot. Here is a basic nymph rig.

Nymph Set-Ups

Experimenting with various combinations of flies on a single leader can be advantageous.

1. Single-fly set-up with a split shot positioned about 4-6 inches above the fly for weight.
2. Two-fly set-up with a larger weighted top fly and a smaller fly, called a dropper, tied off the bend of the first hook, and trailing 8" or more.
3. Three-fly set-up begins with a larger top fly and two smaller flies as droppers, spaced 8" or more.

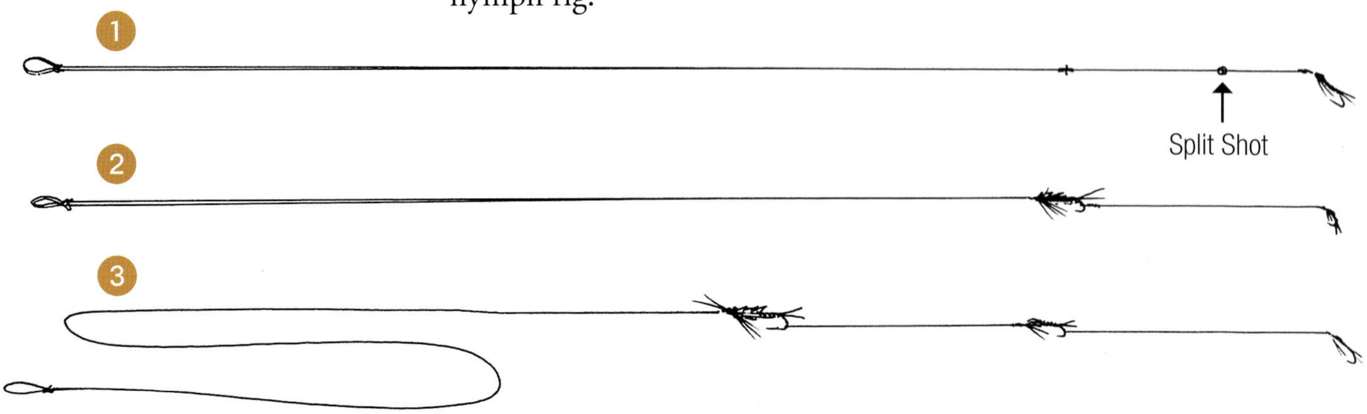

What You Need

A 7.5- to 9-foot rod, floating fly line, 9-foot leader, two feet of tippet, split shot, and a nymph pattern. Additionally, you may want to use a strike indicator. Because nymphs are taken below the surface, it can be difficult to detect when a fish has taken your fly. A strike indicator is a float that is visible to the angler. When the fish strikes your nymph the strike indicator will stop, at which point you can set the hook. Some anglers who choose not to use strike inductors will watch the end of their floating fly line for any indication of a strike.

Presentation Techniques

Nymphs are cast upstream, either straight above the angler or off to the side towards the opposite bank. The goal here is to cast a few feet or more above the suspected lie of the fish so the fly has time to sink before reaching the fish.

Most nymphing is done with a short amount of line, 25-30 feet. This will allow the angler to maintain control of the fly line and ensure the fly is staying on the bottom in dead drift. Two techniques are important here: mending and stripping in line, both of which will be discussed below. One or both of these techniques allow for a natural drift of the fly and keep the fly deep in the fish's zone.

Straight Upstream

You can cast a nymph straight upstream when you are standing in the river and there is productive water above you. Make a short cast just above a suspected lie. After the fly hits the water, line and rig will start to drift towards you. At this point begin stripping in slack line with your line hand at the speed of the current, not pulling on the fly. Let the slack line fall in the water or coil it up in your hand. The nymph will stay deep through the drift. Pick up and recast when you have stripped in the fly line almost to the leader.

Up and Across

Cast your nymph upstream at a 45-degree angle to the shore, five or six feet above a suspected lie. If the currents are even, there will be no need to mend the line; fly line and nymph will drift downriver off to your side. Strip in any slack line to

Up and Across

A good presentation for catching fish directly across stream; perhaps on the bank.

1. Pick line off water and cast to 2.
2. Fly should be positioned above your position in the river.
3. Follow the fly or indicator with your rod tip as it moves downstream, mending when needed.

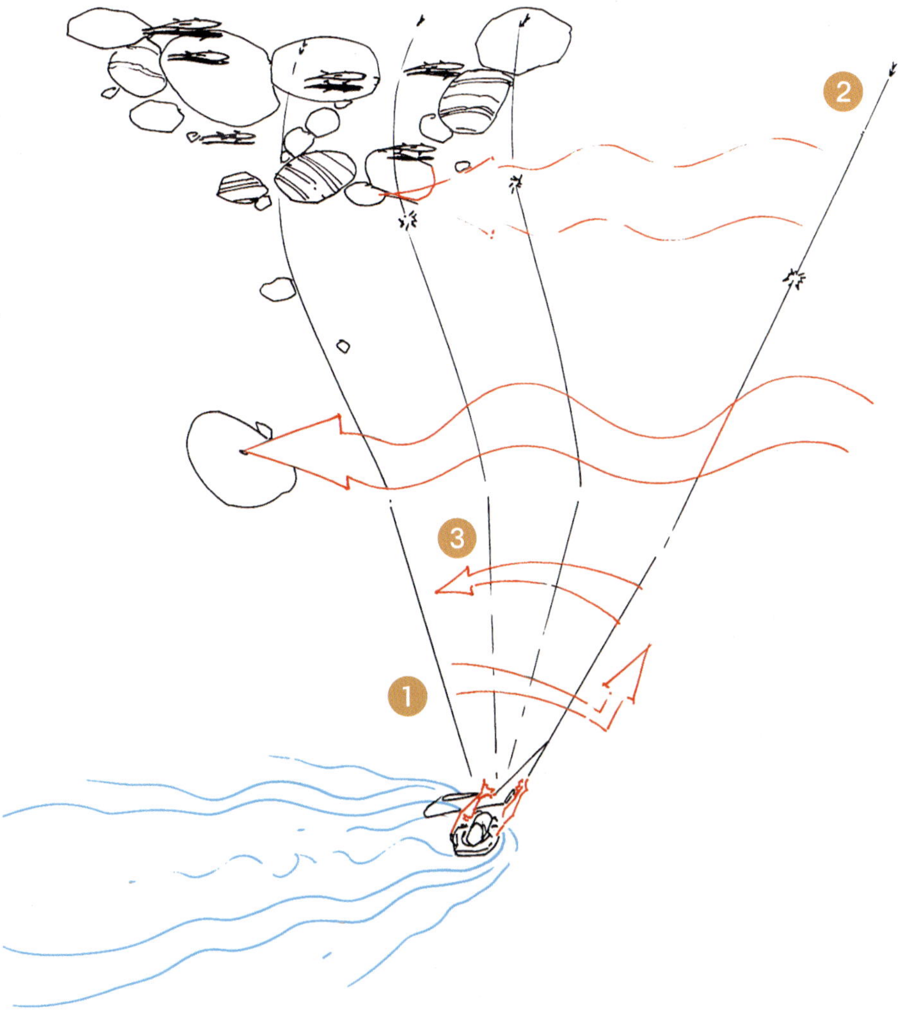

prevent line pulling the fly. When the line reaches your position, pick up fly and recast.

Up, Across and Down

Downstream presentations are effective on spooky fish.

1 Cast to Position 1, following the fly with your rod tip to Position 2.

3 Mend the belly of your fly line, including indicator if necessary, to Position 3.

4 Follow the fly line with your rod tip down stream to maintain a drag-free drift.

Up, Across and Down

This technique is the same as above, but when the line is parallel to your position, extend the drift to fish the water off to your side and below your position. In order to accomplish this, a mend must be incorporated into the drift after the fly passes your position. Mending is defined as repositioning the belly of your fly line on the water to counteract the pull of the fly line on the fly. Mending is accomplished by moving the belly of the fly line above the fly with an authoritative roll or flick of the rod tip. This mend will keep the fly moving with the speed of the current and on the bottom. When the line reaches the end of the drift, pick up fly and recast.

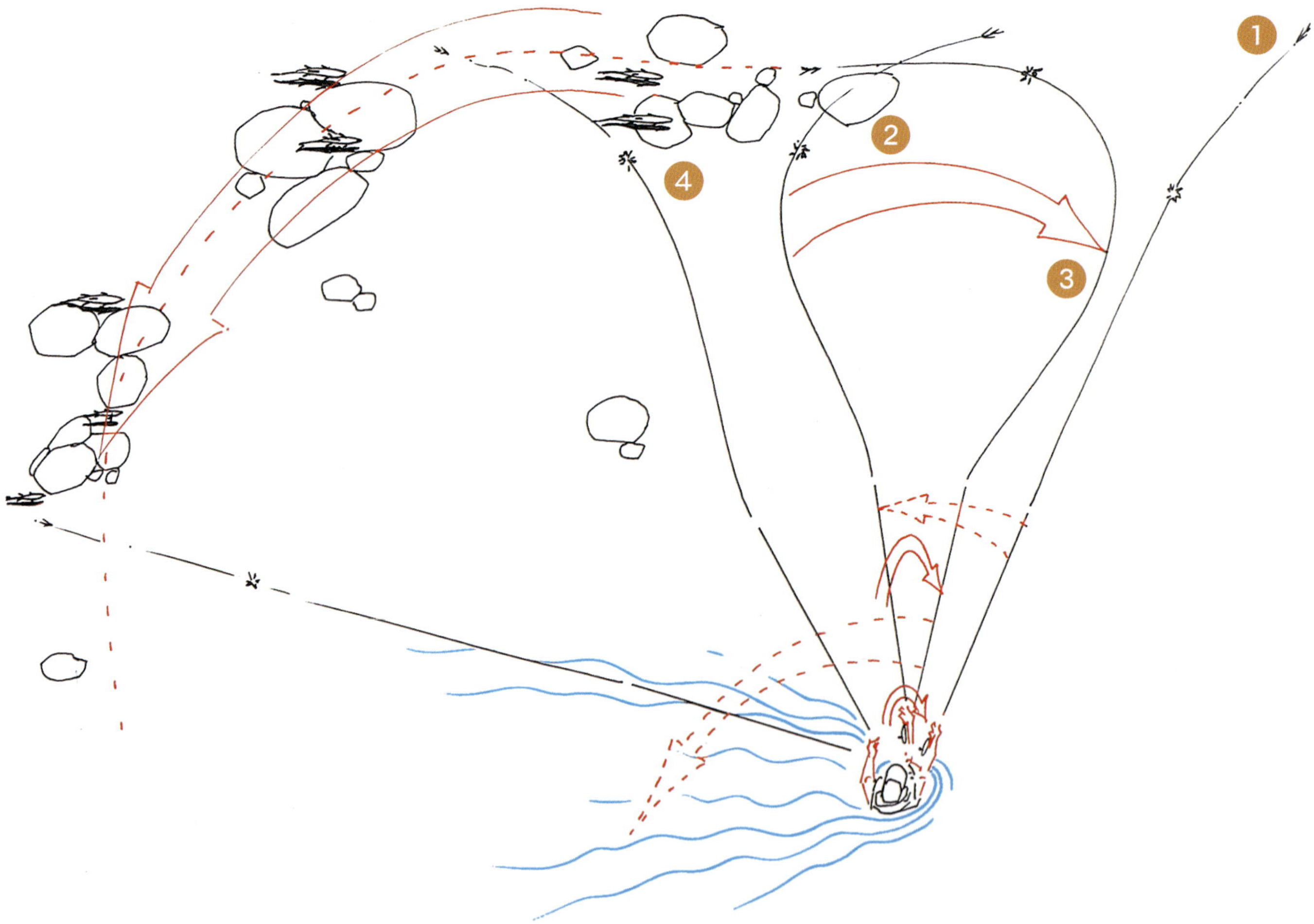

Extending Your Drift

This is a slightly more advanced technique because it requires you to feed slack line into the drift to achieve a longer float below you. Use the same Up, Across and Down technique mentioned above, but after the fly passes your position and begins to drift below you, mend and feed 5 to 6 feet of slack line out of the rod tip. This slack line will allow the nymph to float a longer distance while

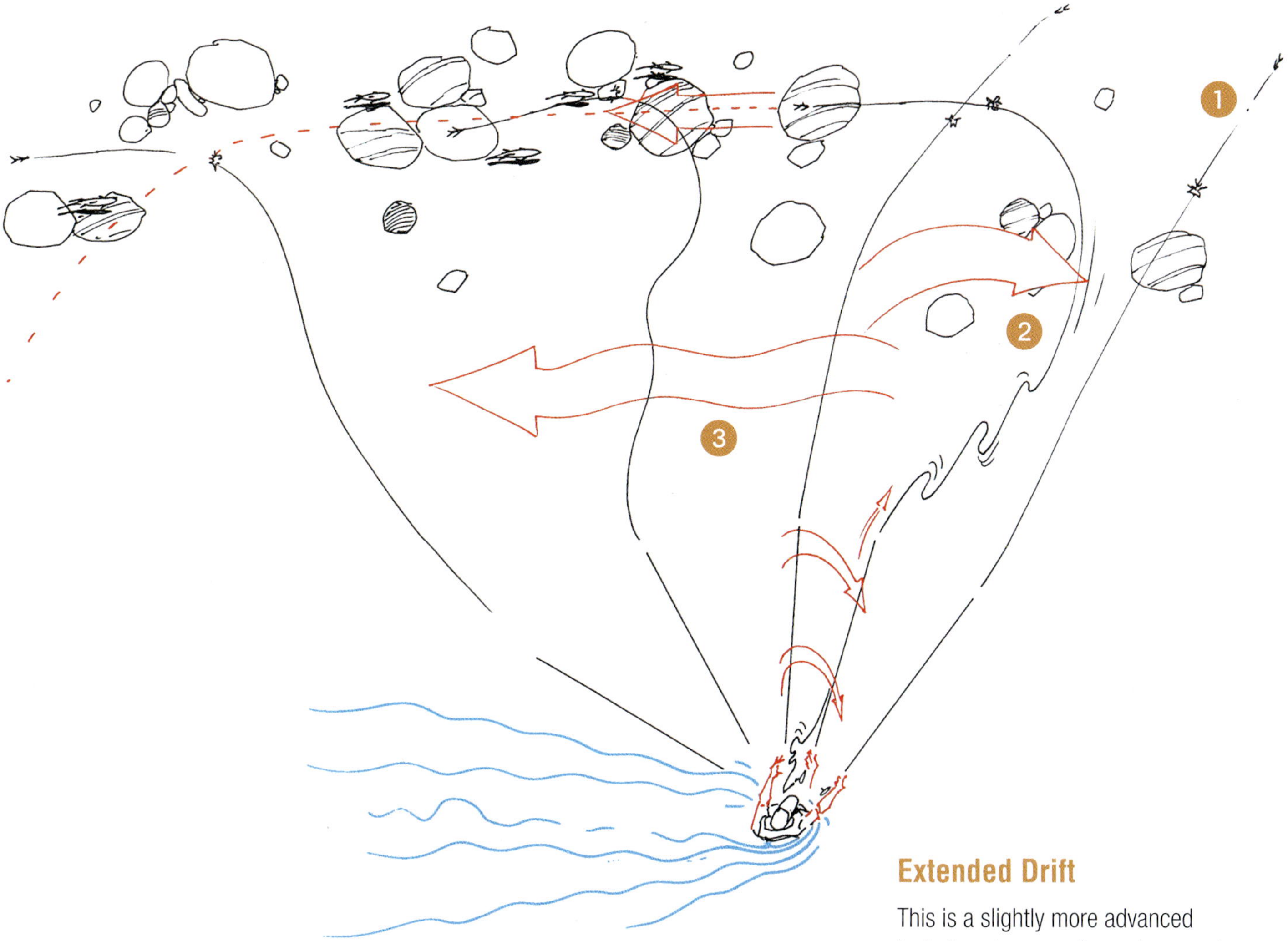

Extended Drift

This is a slightly more advanced technique because it requires you to feed slack line into the drift to achieve a longer float below you.

1 Cast slightly upstream to Position 1.

2 When the line is directly off to the side, mend upstream and throw some coils of slack on top of the water.

3 Follow the drift with your rod tip. Eventually the slack will play out and the line will tighten below you. Note: Detecting a strike with slack on the water can be challenging and requires concentration. Look for any abnormal movement in the end of the fly line such as an upstream movement or sudden stop.

remaining on the bottom. Once the line has been fed, lower your rod and follow the drift with your rod tip until the rod is pointed downriver. If you can perfect this technique there is almost no limit to how far you can extend a drift as long as you learn to feed line without disrupting the position of the fly in the water. Feeding line out of the rod tip must be practiced, and you will develop your own style for doing this. One common technique it to wiggle the rod tip from side to side, feeding out the slack line you have been stripping in.

High-Sticking

This is a variation of an extended drift which requires almost no stripping and no mending. Instead, the rod is used to lift line off the water and then set it back down. Cast up and across, and as the line begins its downstream movement, begin to lift the rod, keeping as much line off the water as you can without pulling the fly towards you. Your rod will be at the highest point when the fly line is directly off to your side. As the fly moves past you, begin lowering the rod tip, placing the fly line back on the water with the speed of the current. When the fly line reaches the end of the drift, pick up the fly and recast.

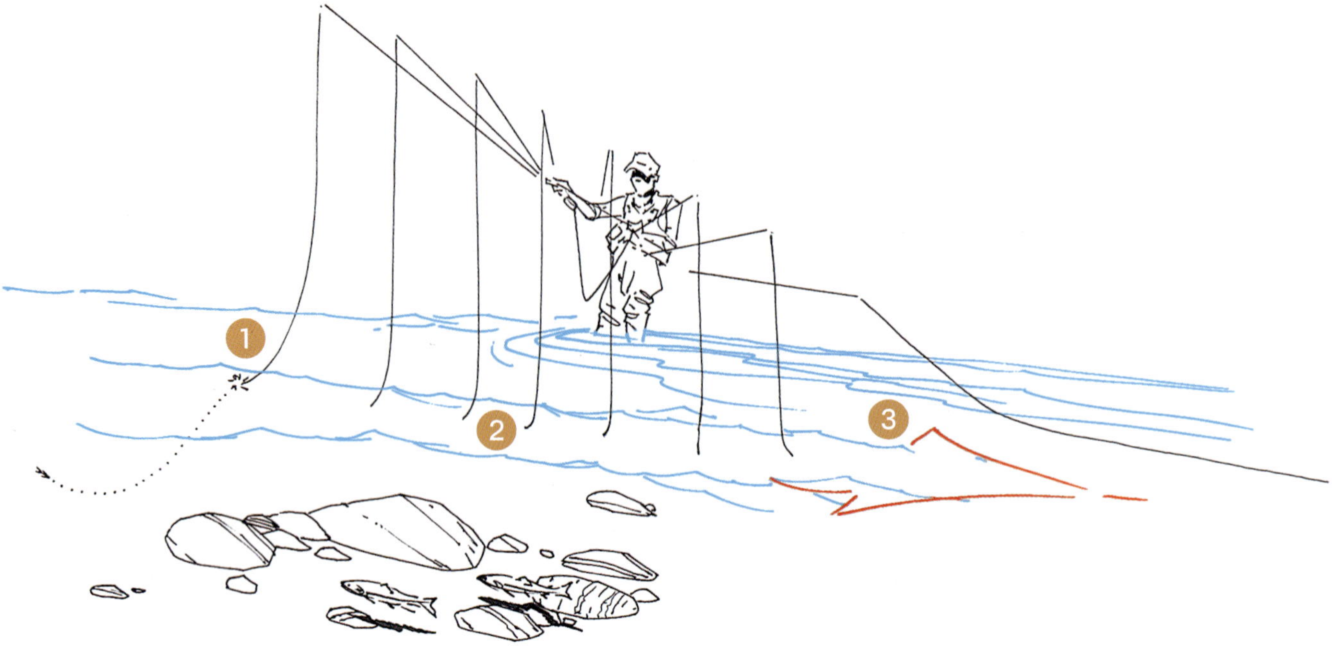

High-Stick Nymphing

Referring to the position of the rod tip above the fly, proper high-sticking combines a short cast, 10-15 feet, so that fly line and some of the butt of the leader can be kept off the water.

1. Make a short cast to Position 1. The rod tip should be held high to keep most, if not all, fly line off the water.
2. Follow the drift with your rod tip keeping fly line off the water.
3. As the fly moves downstream you can gradually lower the rod tip to accommodate the distance the fly moves downstream.

Across and Down

Less effective overall than the above techniques, simply because the fly is not allowed to sink very far, casting downstream to the bank at a 45-degree angle and letting the nymph swing through the bottom currents will frequently take a fish that may be holding near the surface taking emergers. One effective technique is to cast down and across, feed slack line to allow the fly to get a little deeper and then let the fly swing.

Dry Flies

Dry flies are fished on the surface and the strikes, as well as the fly, are visible to the angler. Even if you don't see the fish take the fly, there will be a visible or audible splash. Dry-fly hatches are frequently encountered in riffles, runs and flats because that is where the nymphs live. As a rule, most nymphs will emerge 30-40 feet, sometimes more, below where the nymphs begin their assent to the surface of the water; this is because the nymph needs time to emerge from the nymphal shuck. Some of the best

Catskills Dry Fly

dry-fly fishing occurs at the tail end of a riffle, the start of a run, or in a flat. Likewise, many species of insects return to riffles to lay eggs and die on the surface or drown. Either way, riffles, runs and flats are a great place to prospect with dry flies.

What You Need

A 7 1/2- to 9-foot rod, floating line, 9-foot leader, two feet of tippet, fly floatant, fly-drying patch or fly-drying powder. Although dry flies are constructed with water-shedding materials, most dry flies need to be dressed with specially formulated water-repellant grease in order to maintain buoyancy. After fishing for a while or catching fish, the water-shedding grease will begin to wear off and the flies will need to be dried out and re-greased. If your fly is no longer floating, either tie on a new fly and wait for the old fly to dry, or use a cloth, shirt or specially designed fly-drying patch to compress the water out of the fly. Some anglers use a water-absorbing dry-fly power to dry the fly before it is re-greased. After compressing or drying off the fly,

Across-and-Down Nymphing

One effective technique is to cast down and across, feeding slack line to allow the fly to get a little deeper and then let the fly swing.

1. Cast nymph down and across to Position 1.

2. Feed several coils of slack line immediately into the drift to let the fly sink.

3. Let slack line play out as the fly begins to swing.

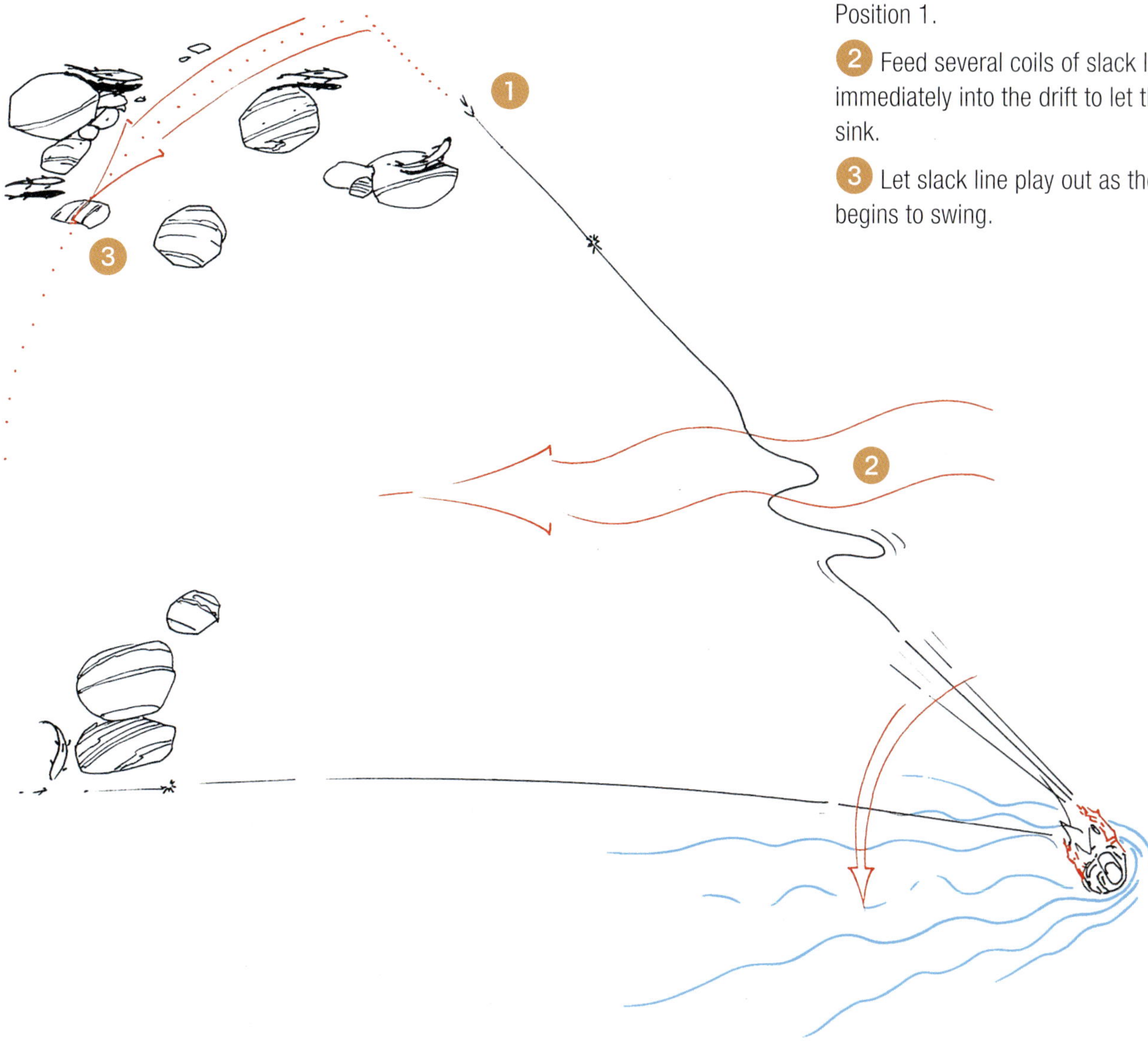

Skeletal remains of hatched stoneflies are common on riverbanks in spring.

blow on it a few times and reapply grease. Most dry flies should last through at least a dozen casts, but most flies need to be dried and redressed after catching a fish.

Presentation Techniques

Riffles and runs are composed of fast, broken water, so the fish's view to the surface is obstructed and trout have to make quick decisions about what to eat. For this reason, fish are less fussy about presentation, and angler errors such as drag are less of a factor for failure. Many strikes are missed in riffles because anglers don't respond fast enough to hook the fish. On the other hand, fish will more frequently hook themselves without the need to set a hook, because the strike is so hard; then the pull of the line is so quick the fish will break-off. In either case, the angler needs to pay attention to the fly and the strike when fishing riffles. Flats are some of the most difficult places to fish dry flies. The smooth, unbroken water surface allows fish to inspect our imitations more carefully. Flats often require exact imitations, finer tippet, longer leaders, and more delicate casts.

Presentation techniques are almost identical to those of nymphing mentioned above: straight upstream; up and across; up, across and down; and extended drifts downstream. Dry flies fished downstream and skated across the surface of the water can also be effective. Many anglers find success fishing dry flies downstream, subsurface. Fishing a dry fly wet is effective in mimicking emerging insects, drowned adults, and adults returning to the water to lay eggs.

Emergers

As their name implies, emergers are representational of emerging insects such as mayflies. Emerging insects encounter great difficulty trying to break through the surface film of the water. A frequent comparison is that of a human trying to push through four to five feet of dirt. Additional problems also occur when the insect is trying to wiggle free from the nymphal shuck in which

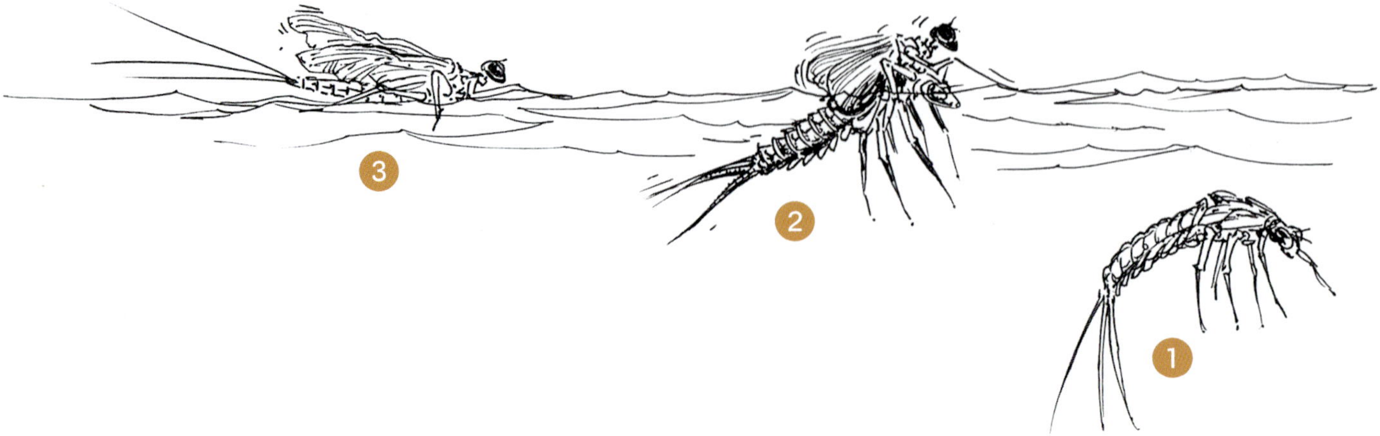

Mayfly Emerger in Surface Film

Mayfly in various stages of emergence.

1 Emerging nymph floating or swimming to the surface.

2 Emerging adult mayfly splitting the nymphal shuck.

3 Drifting adult: This is the newly emerged mayfly adult ready to unfold its wings and fly off to nearby vegetation.

it sometimes gets trapped. Some insects may be born crippled or even stillborn, and in both cases may never make the complete transformation to adult. These insects are very vulnerable to trout, who feed on them with regularity.

What You Need

Same equipment as for dry-fly fishing.

Emerger patterns such as a Quigley Cripple or Floating Nymph are designed to suspend in the surface film or just below the surface to mimic the emerging insect. These flies may have a component such as a wing or ball of yarn that can be dressed with floatant, while the body of the fly is intended to get wet and suspend below the surface.

Presentation Techniques

The techniques for fishing emergers are the same as with a dry fly, floating line on a nine-foot leader. Upstream; up and across; up, across and down are all effective provided there is a drag-free drift.

Wet Flies

Wet flies refers to a specific type of fly which is a soft hackle, winged wet, or flymph. Wet fly-fishing dates back to the origins of fly-fishing and is probably how fly-fishing began. Today we think of wet flies more specifically as either caddis pupae, drowned or swimming mayflies or caddisflies. They are fished in a swimming style similar to streamers, which will be talked about later. Although any of the above techniques can be used with wet flies, the action we are after is that of a swimming insect. Thus there are a few established techniques specifically designed for wet flies, and a majority of these require a down-and-across presentation.

"When you have made your cast . . . you are no longer a careless observer. As you mend the cast and work your fly well down . . . through the cold water, your whole mind is with it, picturing its drift, guiding its swing, holding it where you know he will be. And when the shock of his take jars through to your forearms and you lift the rod to its bend, you know that in a moment the strength of his leaping body will shatter the water to brilliance, however dark the day."

—Roderick Haig-Brown, A River Never Sleeps *(1946)*

Mayfly Emerger

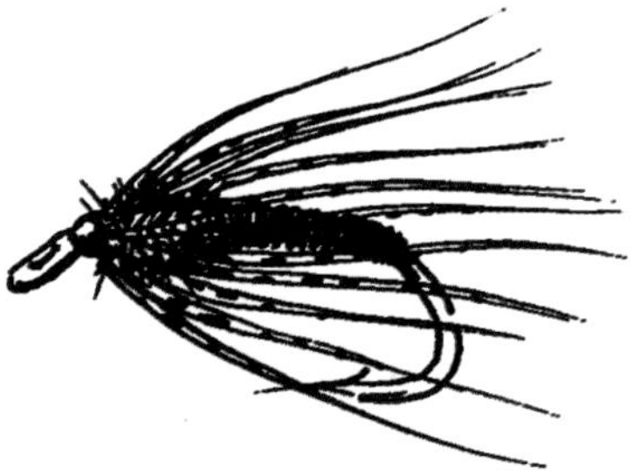

Wet Fly

Caddis Pupa Emerger

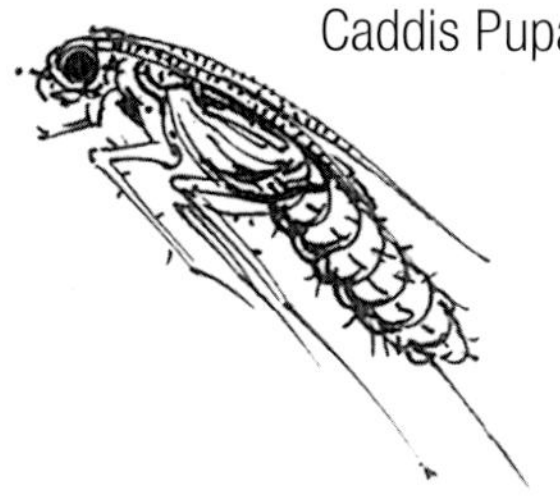

What you need

Same equipment as dry-fly fishing. Alternatively, wet flies can be fished with a sinking or sink-tip line in deeper waters such as runs or pools. One of my favorite ways to fish wets in flatter, deeper sections of a river is on a clear intermediate full-sinking or sink-tip line. Sink tip lines are a little easier to manage than full-sinking lines, which are impossible to mend once the line breaks the surface of the water.

Presentation Techniques

Classic Wet Fly Swing: Cast your fly either across the current or downstream at a 45-degree angle to the bank. Place one upstream mend in the line to prevent the fly from swinging too fast through the current. If you mend properly, the fly will be facing upstream as it swings through the current. Lower your rod and follow the swing of the fly with your rod tip until it straightens out below you. Strip the fly back upstream to your position or pick up the fly and repeat the cast.

Classic Wet-Fly Swing

1 Cast your fly either across the current or downstream at a 45-degree angle to the bank.

2 Place one upstream mend in the line to prevent the fly from swinging too fast through the current. If you mend properly, the fly will be facing upstream as it swings through the current.

3 Lower your rod and follow the swing of the fly with your rod tip until it straightens out below you. Strip the fly back upstream to your position or pick up the fly and repeat the cast.

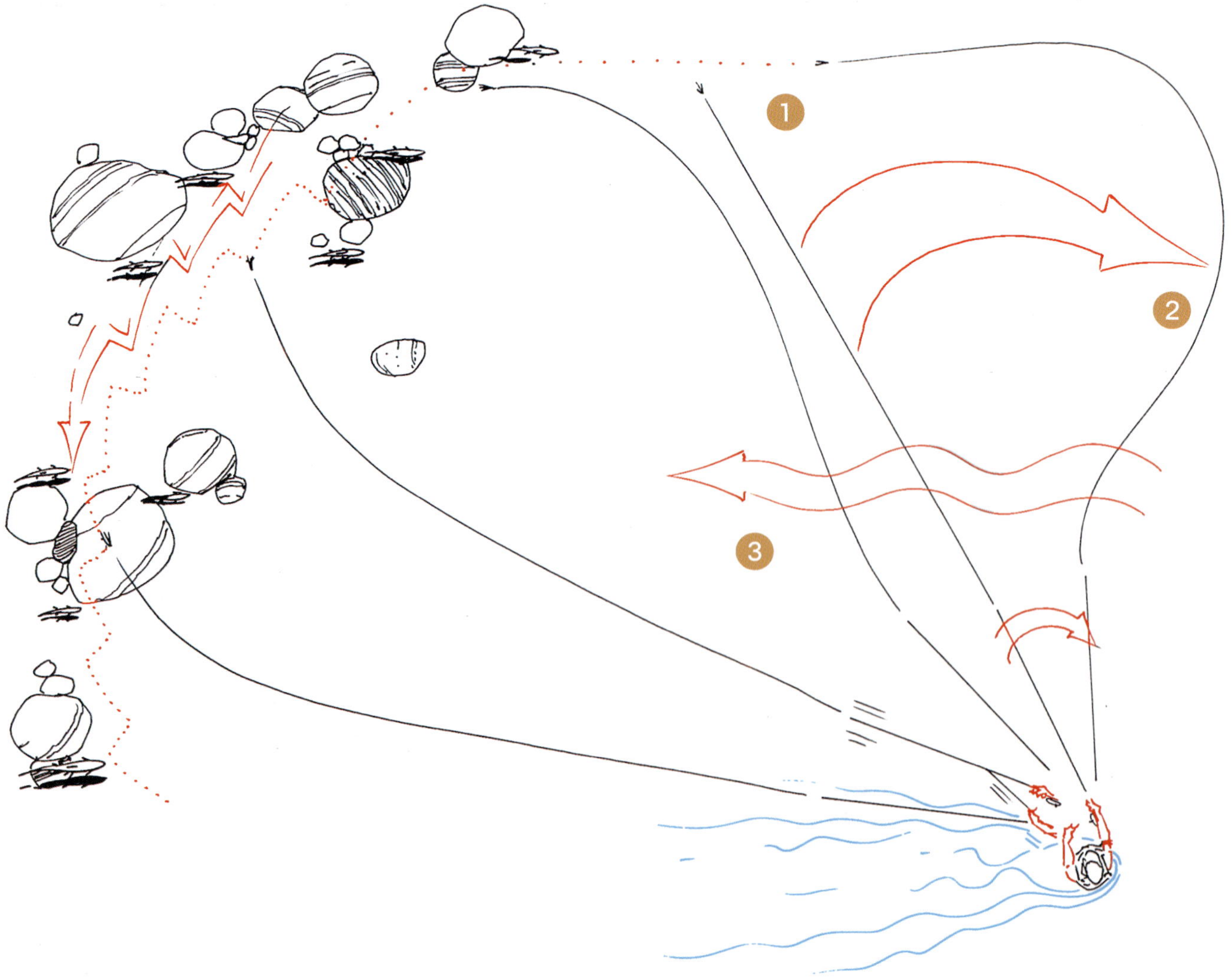

I use two variations to enhance the classic wet-fly swing. After the mend, I feed a few feet of slack line into the drift to enable the fly to sink a little deeper before it catches the current and swings. When the fly is swinging I will impart tiny twitches to the fly by pumping the rod tip or tugging on the fly line in my line hand. Thus, as the fly swings it actually pulsates through the water; I have found very few fish that can resist a pulsating fly. Strikes while fishing this method can be jolting, and many fish will break off because you are fishing a tight line.

Strip Method

This is a more active method of swinging the fly through and across the current. Cast to the bank or slightly upstream and mend the belly of the line upstream. As the fly drifts downriver, impart two-, three- and four-inch strips at five- to ten-second intervals, stripping the fly back to you. If done correctly the fly will be both swinging and facing broadside to the current. To help maintain the fly's broadside position, follow the fly's path with your rod tip.

Strip Method

A more active method of swinging the fly through and across the current.

1. Cast fly across and down to Position 1.
2. Mend belly of fly line to Position 2.
3. Follow the fly with the rod tip, maintaining a tight line and strip the fly across the current at varying intervals.

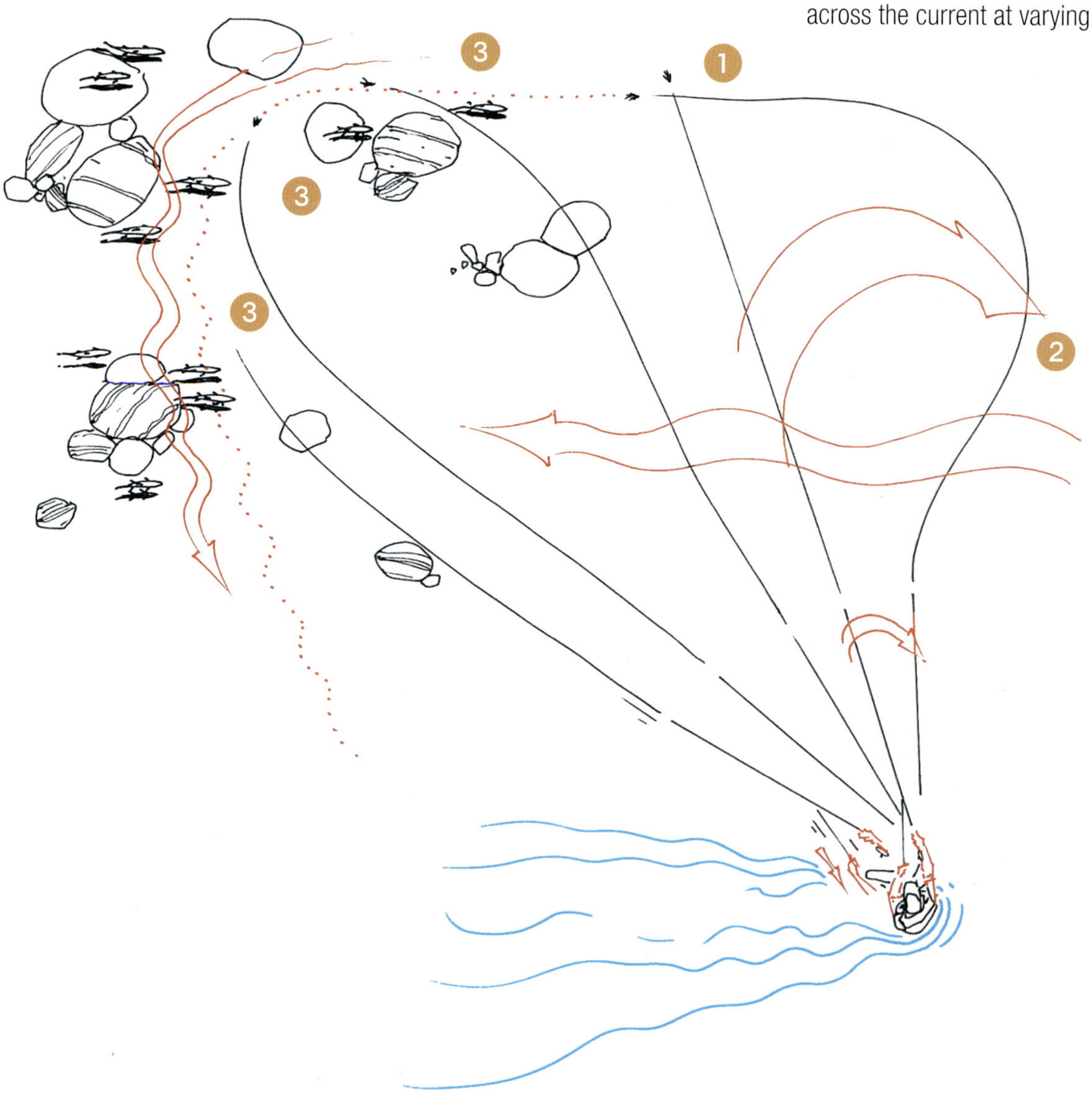

Downstream Mend

This is a fast-swinging fly, giving the fish a side profile of the fly, and usually will take the most aggressive fish in the river.

1 Cast the fly to the bank and mend the fly line downstream.

2 The fly line will pull the fly first downstream and then across the current below you.

Downstream Mend

This technique should be used with some discretion, because it will only take a certain percentage of fish particularly at spawning times or in spring when fish are more aggressive. Cast the fly to the bank and mend the fly line downstream. The fly line will pull the fly first downstream and then across the current below you. This is a fast-swinging fly and will usually take the most aggressive fish in the river.

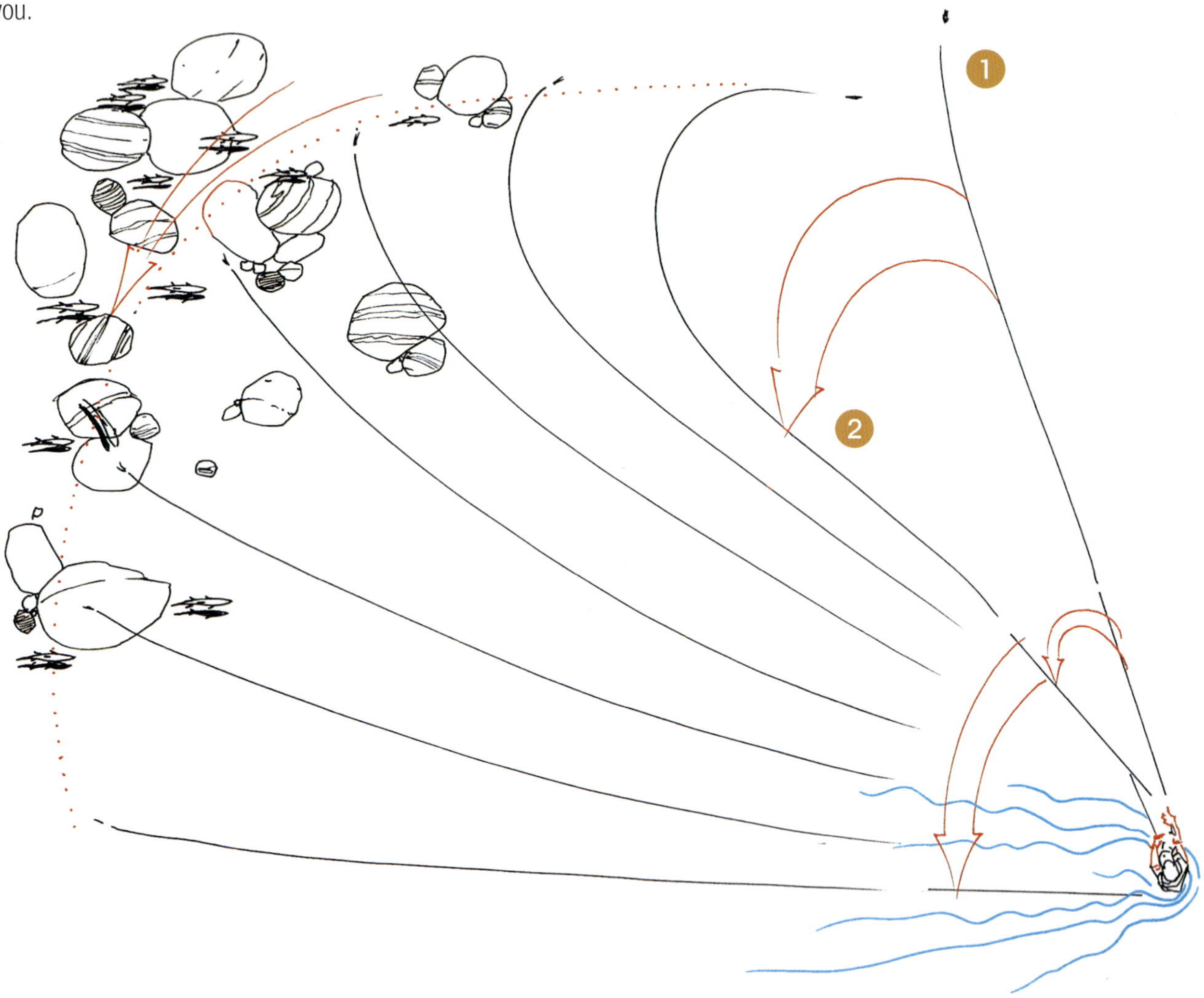

Leisenring Lift

The Leisenring Lift is named after angler James Leisenring. He developed this style of fishing for visible feeding fish that refused to take a dry fly. Cast your fly approximately eight to ten feet above the feeding fish, and follow the drift of the fly with your rod tip to reduce drag and let your fly achieve some depth prior to reaching the fish. When you think the fly is just ahead of the fish, begin to lift your rod tip, pulling the fly thought the water column to the surface. The fish will see the fly rising to the surface and rise up and catch the fly.

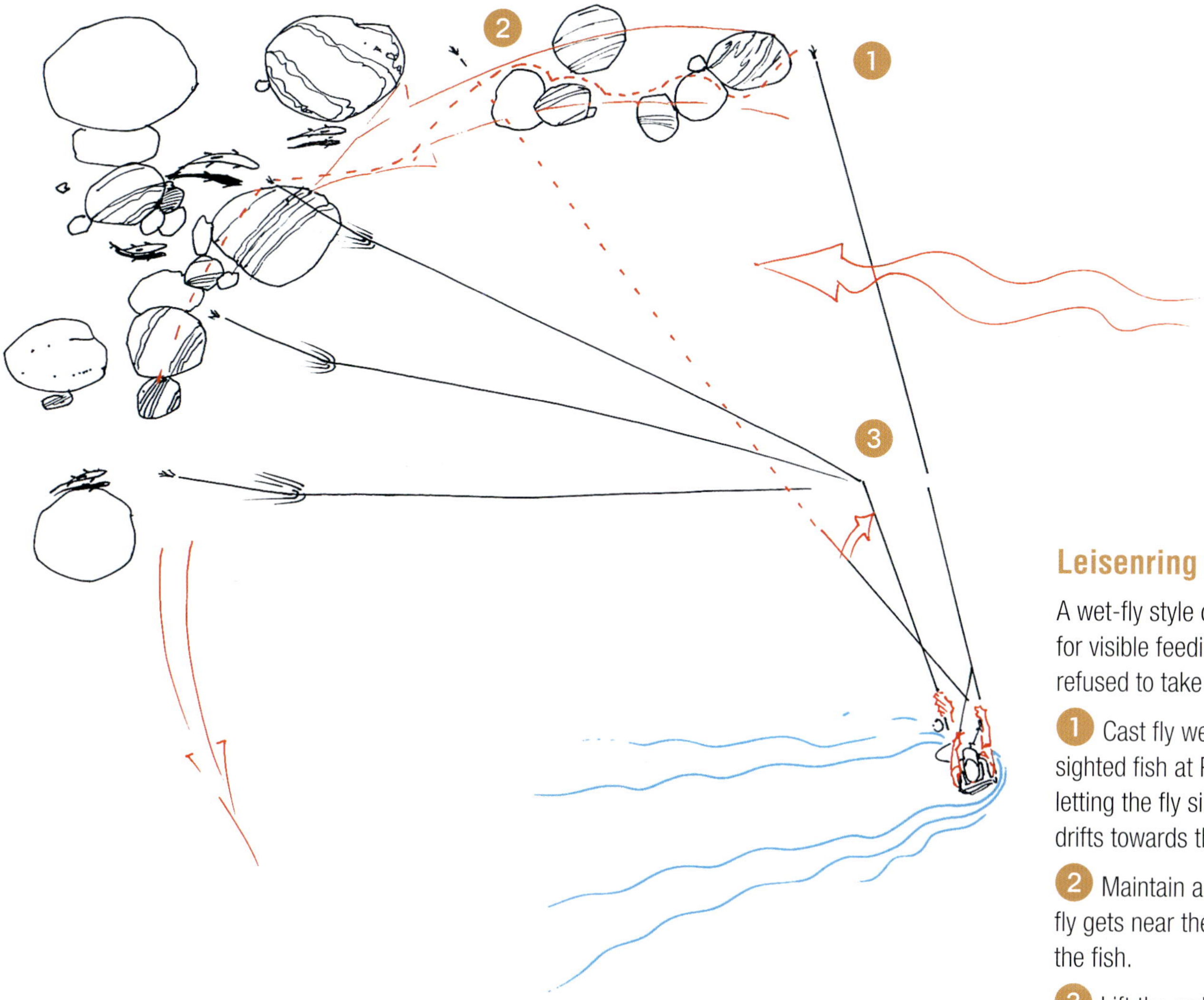

Leisenring Lift

A wet-fly style of fishing for visible feeding fish that refused to take a dry fly.

1. Cast fly well above a sighted fish at Position 1, letting the fly sink deep as it drifts towards the fish.
2. Maintain a swing until the fly gets near the position of the fish.
3. Lift the rod tip, raising the fly in the water column in front of the fish.

Induced Take

Similar to the Leisenring Lift, the induced take is another method of getting the fly to rise in front of the fish. Here, the fly is fished shallow. Cast five or six feet in front of a rising fish and position your rod tip upstream and low to the water. As the fly line tightens, the fly will rise to the surface, inducing the fish to strike.

Streamers

Steamers are representative of small baitfish, leeches, crayfish, and other large food items that are agile swimmers. Streamers are frequently large and contain many long feathers, animal hair, or synthetic materials that give the impression of movement and pulsation in the water. Streamers also come in a more expressive range of colors than most flies to match the glittering and colorful bands on the sides of baitfish. Considered attractor patterns, streamers are suggestive imitations that represent a variety of different food forms. Aggressive fish will chase down a streamer, and the takes can be voracious.

Aggressive fish will chase down a streamer, and the takes can be voracious.

However, it is not the agile swimmers that get a trout's attention; it is the erratic swimmers, the ones that appear wounded, helpless or in a panic, that draw trout. Trout focus on these vulnerabilities of their prey. For this reason streamers are often fished with a lot of movement, involving the both rod and line hand.

Do not underestimate the use of streamers, especially as a searching pattern for exploring unfamiliar waters. The most popular of all streamers, the Wolly Bugger, is often the first pattern I try on any river. These flies are so effective that I can always find some fish, and often larger fish, than if I start with dry flies, wets, or nymphs.

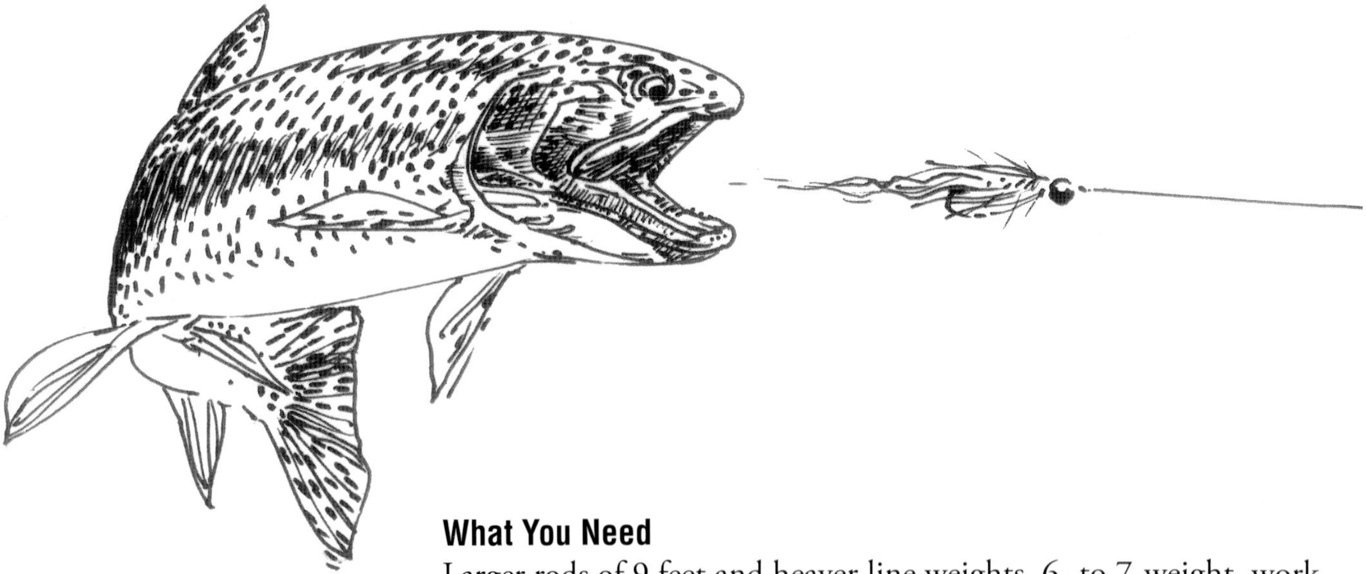

What You Need

Larger rods of 9 feet and heaver line weights, 6- to 7-weight, work best for casting these sometimes large and heavy flies. Streamers can be fished on floating, sinking, or sink-tip lines. Streamers are generally fished in deeper waters, and a sinking or sink-tip line will keep a fly at the fish's depth longer than a floating line. Some anglers who do not like sinking line may use an extra-long leader, 15-20 feet, to keep the fly down. If using a sinking or sink-tip line you can use a much shorter leader, 3-5 feet. A shorter leader will allow the fly to sink faster with the fly line.

Craig Schuhmann

This trout succumbed to a small Black Leech stripped along a submerged weed bed.

Presentation Techniques

All the methods listed for wet-fly fishing are suitable for streamers, but, as mentioned before, the retrieve is aggressive. One thing is certain about streamer-fishing: you can never retrieve a fly so fast that a fish will not be able to catch it. Fish are incredibly responsive and react with stunning speed when they are excited.

The secret to good streamer-fishing is inducing a strike with an active retrieve. Streamer-fishing is rarely pretty and never delicate. Streamers enter the water with a loud splash and then the fly is jerked back to the angler. When the proper retrieve allows the feathers or hair to pulsate in the water the fly is said to be "activated". Too fast or too slow of a retrieve may deaden the action of the fly, which is undesirable. Likewise, a steady retrieve without pauses will deaden the action of the fly. Go erratic, and work the streamer like a wounded baitfish with a lot of stops, starts, and movements of the rod tip.

One thing is certain about streamer-fishing: you can never retrieve a fly so fast that a fish will not be able to catch it.

Jerk-Strip Retrieve

This method is so named because it uses both the rod and the stripping hand to bring the fly in quickly. Cast the fly across or downstream, allow it to sink for a few seconds, and then retrieve with alternating pulls from the rod tip and the line hand. You can also shake the rod tip a few times and then strip line with your hand, or shake the rod tip as you strip line with your hand.

Line-Strip Retrieve: Cast the fly to the bank and with rod tip pointed at the fly begin a retrieve with your line hand. There are many retrieve styles and some may work better than others. Here are some examples:

1. Sequence of one-foot pulls, followed by a 2- to 3-second pause.
2. One long pull, followed by a couple 3- to 4-inch pulls, followed by 2- to 3-second pause.
3. Short, 1- to 2-inch pulls, in groups of one to four, followed by a pause. In other words: strip, pause; strip, strip, pause; strip, strip, strip, pause; strip, pause; etc.

Swing Method

Same as the wet-fly swing, cast to the bank at a 45-degree angle, mend the belly of the fly line upstream and let the fly swing through the current.

Upstream Strip

Cast the fly directly upstream or up and to the side. In order to give the fly the appropriate action, this technique requires a fast strip because the current will immediatly drift the fly downstream. The strip should be slow enough that the fly is allowed to sink, but fast enough to give it action.

Upstream Dead Drift

Same as dead-drifting nymphs. This is an effective technique in deeper runs. I always add the occasional twitch to the drifting fly.

Hang-Down

In the right conditions, such as fishing from a boat when you can position yourself in the middle of a pool or flat, this technique is deadly. The fly is swung or cast downstream and then allowed to hang down straight below the angler, wiggling in the current. Action is imparted to the fly with the occasional twitch, small strip, or moving your rod side to side, but essentially the fly sits in one spot. Strikes are furious because of the tight line, and break-offs are common.

Striking, Playing and Landing a Fish

Ugggh! If you hear this exclamation on a river it can only mean two things, either someone just broke a critical piece of equipment or they lost a fish. Sometimes both happen at once. It is a part of fishing, and nothing will leave an indelible impression in the mind of an angler quite like losing a fish, especially a big one. Those of us who are truly obsessed may never get it out of our minds. We are forced to wrestle with the event in our sleep or relive it while sharing our story with other anglers. Some of us may return to the exact spot the next day to regain our dignity by hooking and catching the same fish. Such is our pathology.

Regardless, striking, playing and landing a fish is a learned skill that will increase with the more fish you catch. Understanding and inspecting your equipment has a lot to do with success in this area. Check your knots, do not use damaged or cheap fly lines and leaders, and always inspect your hooks for sharpness. If you use a reel with a drag system, set it loose until you can fine-tune it to the size of fish you are catching. Most importantly, try to gauge how much tension should be applied with the rod when setting the hook. Below are a few guidelines to help guide you in the learning process.

Detecting a strike and setting the hook can only occur with limited slack line. The more direct connection to the fish we have through our equipment, the greater chance we have of success.

Striking or the Hook-Set

How trout ingest a fly is something of a mystery even to scientists; we are not entirely sure how they do it. Despite this lack of knowledge, trout do take our flies and they can spit them out just as fast. This is why it is important to detect a strike as soon as it occurs. Detecting a strike and setting the hook can only occur with limited slack line. The more direct connection to the fish we have through our equipment, the greater chance we have of success. When we detect a fish has taken our fly, the first action is to remove slack and put tension on the line by raising the rod tip and putting a bend in the rod. How hard we raise the rod tip depends on the size of fly and size of fish. Small flies and likewise delicate tippet require a delicate hook-set, otherwise we may break the tippet or fly, or pull it out of the fish's mouth. Larger fish, larger flies, and larger tippet all require a slightly stronger hook-set to send the hook into the jaw of the fish. Frequently, fish will hook themselves, and in this case there is little that needs to be done by the angler except to keep tension on the line.

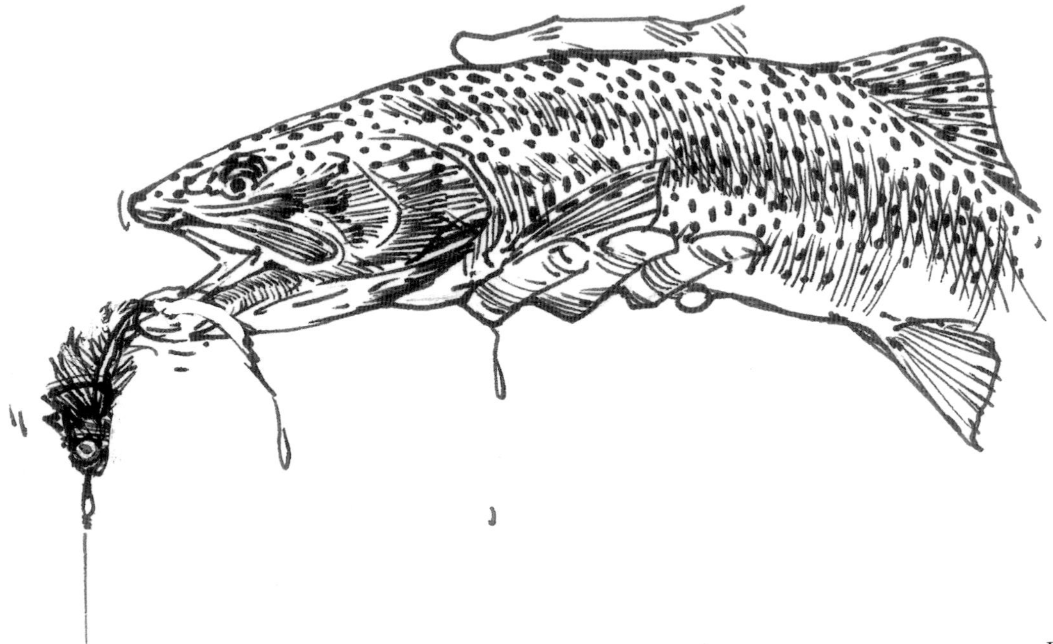

Playing a Fish

Once the hook is set and you can feel the fish, you must keep the rod tip high for the entire fight. Small fish do not require much force and they can be reeled in or stripped in with your line hand. If you feel the fish pulling excessively against the line, such that your rod tip wants to drop to the water, let the fish take line, keep the rod tip high, and don't allow any slack to develop in the line.

Larger fish will require more finesse and most often have to be played off the reel. In other words, when a larger fish is hooked, try and get all loose line onto the reel, then play the fish with the bend of the rod, keeping the rod tip high and letting the fish strip line off the reel. When the fish begins to take line off the reel, this is called a run. Let the fish run, and when it stops or tires, begin reeling in slack line until the next run. You'll know the fish is tiring when you can reel in the fish and there are no more runs.

Once the hook is set and you can feel the fish, you must keep the rod tip high for the entire fight.

Let the fish run, and when it stops or tires, begin reeling in slack line until the next run.

Landing a Fish

More fish are lost trying to land them than at any other time. This occurs for a couple of reasons. The fish can be difficult to reach with a long rod. In order to bring the fish to your feet you have to move the rod off to the side and behind you. Sometimes moving the rod in this way can put pressure on the fish and it may begin to thrash. If you're unprepared to give it line it could break off.

In order to bring the fish to your feet you have to move the rod off to the side and behind you.

Never reel your line so far onto the reel that the leader knot goes into the guides. This knot will invariably catch in a guide, resulting in a lost fish or broken rod tip. Instead, reel in just short of the knot and use the rod to leverage the fish to your feet. Here, a net will come in handy, extending your reach to the fish.

If you do not have a net, try to brace the fish against your leg and cradle the fish's belly in your hand. Remove the hook with your free hand and let the fish swim away.

Catch-and-Release Fishing

If you do not intend to keep fish, land and release the fish with as little trauma as possible. Here are some effective guidelines for catch-and-release fishing.

1. Use barbless hooks.
2. Play the fish and land it as quickly as possible.
3. Always use a net. This ensures a quick landing, and you never have to touch the fish.
4. Do not touch the fish if you do not have to. If you do touch the fish, use wet hands or specially designed fish gloves. Handle the fish in the net if possible. Of course, we all want pictures. Do this quickly, within seconds after taking the fish out of the water. Remove the hook from the fish while it is in the water or the net. Angled or specially designed forceps with a hook-releasing mechanism are the best and fastest way.
5. Do not throw the fish back into the water. Instead, cradle the fish in the net or your hand with a loose grip and let the fish swim away under its own power. If the fish is particularly tired, it may take a minute or two for the fish to revive.

Index

Index

Suggested Reading

There are so many good books and DVD's about fly-fishing that I could not possibly list them all here. Instead, I offer a few choice selections by contemporary writers that will inspire and help you build your library. As for the rest of the great books, you will have to discover those on your own.

Curtis Creek Manifesto. Anderson, Sheridan. (Frank Amato Publications, 1978, revised).
A cult classic that has been passed down from generation to generation since its publication. One of the bestselling basic fly-fishing guides on the market. Material is dated, but it contains all the essential concepts in an easy-to-understand graphic style. Great for kids and visual learners.

Trout and Salmon of North America. Behnke, Robert J. (Free Press, 2002).
Beautifully illustrated and authoritative, this reference work covers the life histories and fishing information on over 70 species from steelhead and salmon to trout.

Anatomy of a Trout Stream. Hafele, Rick. (Scientific Angling Mastery Series).
An entomologist's view of a trout's ecosystem. This is a comprehensive DVD combining methods of presentation, insect identification, fly selection, locating trout in a river, and reading water. Should be owned by every angler regardless of expertise.

Nymph-Fishing Rivers and Streams: A Biologist's View of Taking Trout Below the Surface. Hafele, Rick. (Stackpole Books, 2006).
As an entomologist, Rick helps us penetrate the hidden world of insects and trout and gives justification to why these techniques work from the trout's point of view. Simply the best basic nymph-fishing guide on the market.

Handbook of Hatches: Introductory Guide to the Foods Trout Eat & the Most Effective Flies to Match Them. Hughes, Dave. (Stackpole Books; 2 edition. January 2005).
In this easy-to-read guide, Dave teaches how to identify insects and match them to effective patterns.

The Essence of Fly Casting. Krieger, Mel. (Countryman Press, 2001).
Both the book and companion DVD are superb introductions to the West Coast style of casting. Mel's poetic and creative approach to teaching fly-casting will enable you to grasp the basics in no time. For different approaches to casting, see books and videos by Joan Wulff and Lefty Kreh.

Bugwater. Thomason, Arlen. (Stackpole, 2010)
A great entomolgy primer which shows in great photographic detail the hidden life of aquatic insects. Insect life cycles, fly selection and presentation methods are all discussed.

Trout and Their Food: A Compact Guide for Fly Fishers. Whitlock, Dave. (Skyhorse Publishing, 2010). Through easy to understand text and illustrations one can learn in-depth information about the many different food forms in a trout's diet and how to imitate them with flies. Written by one of the great anglers and fly designers of all time.

Advanced Reading

Wet Flies: Tying and Fishing Soft-Hackles, Winged and Wingless Wets, and Fuzzy Nymphs. Hughes, Dave. (Stackpole, 1995).
Concerns all aspects of fishing the wet fly, from fly tying to presentation techniques.Technical reading for the novice reader, but a great primer on the very effective use of wet flies.

Slack Line Strategies for Fly Fishing. Judy, John. (Stackpole Books, 2002).
This is a technical fly-fishing book detailing John's unique approach to presentation for difficult water. Very helpful tips for both novice and expert anglers. Very highly recommended!

Modern Streamers for Trophy Trout: New Techniques, Tactics and Patterns. Linsenman, Bob. (Countryman Press, 2004). Deserves a place on any fly-fishing book list because few authors have covered, in-depth, the art of streamer-fishing for trout.Valuable to both the fly tier and angler.

For other advanced reading material see *Spring Creeks* by Mike Lawson, *Learning from the Water* by Rene Harrop, and *Caddisflies* by Gary LaFontaine.

The Trout and the Fly: A New Approach. Clarke, Brain and John Goddard. (Nick Lyons Books, 1980).
A scientific approach with original research to help the angler understand trout behavior, perceptions and vision. A remarkable, but advanced book that remains widely read after 30 years since its publication.

Stillwater Presentation. Rickards, Denny. (A Stillwater Production, 2010). Should you find yourself drawn to lakes, there is no better book than this one for learning the fundamentals of lake fishing.

Fly Fishing Literature

Trout Bum. Gierach, John. (Simon & Schuster Publishing, 1988).
A selection of humorous and educational stories that typify the fly-fishing experience. It's hard to read this book without wanting to run out of the house and start fishing.

Habits of Rivers. Leeson, Ted. (Lyons Press, 1996)
A contemporary classic in fly-fishing literature. Masterfully written essays that stimulate reflection and inspire philosophical speculation. A rare book that captures the true spirit of the sport.

More Popular Books
from Frank Amato Publications

One of the most enjoyable aspects of fly-fishing is the challenge; however, insect hatches are often downright mystifying. These hatch guides, by some of the most respected experts in the fields of entomology and fly-fishing, will take away some of the guesswork and frustration, leaving you more time for fishing!

Hatch Guide for New England Streams
by Thomas Ames, Jr.

SB: $19.95
ISBN-13: 978-1-57188-210-3
UPC: 0-66066-00424-6

Hatch Guide for Western Streams
by Jim Schollmeyer

196 pages
SB: $19.95
ISBN-13: 978-1-57188-109-0
UPC: 0-66066-00303-4

Now Available as an IPhone APP too!

Hatch Guide for Lakes
by Jim Schollmeyer

SB: $19.95
ISBN-13: 978-1-57188-324-7
UPC: 0-81127-00158-3

Steelhead Fly Angling
by Michael Gorman

This book is a fun-to-read technical manual based on the author's 30-plus years of successes and mistakes while pursuing steelhead, as an angler and a guide. *Steelhead Fly Angling* will shave years off your learning curve. Even if you're a steelhead veteran, you will find strategies that will add to your success.

Flies, techniques, equipment—all the basics are covered. Then Gorman takes it a step further by giving you invaluable *real-world* tactics for overcoming the many challenges that can get in the way of your steelheading success—crowded rivers, rude anglers, your own frustration and impatience, lack of knowledge and skills, changing river conditions, temperamental steelhead . . . Catching steelhead consistently requires planning and preparation for all possibilities. *Steelhead Fly Angling* shows you how to deal with any combination of challenges and, most importantly, formulate a strategic game plan to effectively deal with them. All you've got to lose is years of frustration.
8 1/2 x 11 inches, 188 pages, all color.

SB: $29.95
ISBN-13: 978-1-57188-479-4
UPC: 0-81127-00321-1

HB: $45.00
ISBN-13: 978-1-57188-485-5
UPC: 0-81127-00330-3

Ask for these books at your local fly/tackle shop or call toll-free to order:
1-800-541-9498 (8-5 p.s.t.) • www.AmatoBooks.com

More Popular Books
from Frank Amato Publications

Hatch Guide for Upper Midwest Streams
by Ann R. Miller

In the user-friendly format of the series, Miller discusses the naturals and their behaviors then provides matching fly patterns and fishing techniques on the opposite page. Fly tying is a combination of art and science; fly tiers understand the biology and behavior of an insect, and then imitate it artistically. Color, size, silhouette, and behavior of an artificial are essential, which is why it's important to have some knowledge of the local insects. Mayflies, stoneflies, caddisflies, lesser insects, and crustaceans of the upper Midwest are covered in this book.

Learning to identify insects can be daunting for anyone, but doing so will pay off for you with more fish. Or . . . you can just get this book! 4 x 6 inches, 348 pages, all-color.

SB: $29.95
ISBN-13: 978-1-57188-481-7
UPC: 0-81127-00323-5

Which Fly Do I Use?
by Darren Banasch

5 1/2 x 8 1/2, 48 pages, all color

SB: $8.95
ISBN-13: 978-1-57188-202-8
UPC: 0-66066-00416-1

The Benchside Introduction to Fly Tying
by Ted Leeson & Jim Schollmeyer

Following the incredible success of *The Fly Tier's Benchside Reference*, Jim & Ted now offer the first beginner's book of fly tying to allow readers simultaneous access to fly recipes, tying steps, and techniques. The first 50 pages of this oversized, spiral-bound book are filled with impeccably photographed fly-tying techniques. The next 150 pages are cut horizontally across the page. The top pages show tying steps for dozens of fly patterns, including references to tying techniques that are explained step by step in the bottom pages. Over 1500 beautiful color photographs, 9 x 12 inches, 190 all-color pages.

SPIRAL HB: $45.00
ISBN-13: 978-1-57188-369-8
UPC: 0-81127-00203-0

Bluegill Fly Fishing & Flies
by Terry & Roxanne Wilson

Everyone has a bluegill story. Their yanking, diving, twisting battles make for a tenacious opponent. With their combined 75 years of experience fishing for bluegills, the Wilsons have written the definitive book. 6 x 9 inches, 151 pages, color insert.

SB: $16.95
ISBN-13: 978-1-57188-176-2
UPC: 0-66066-00378-2

Ask for these books at your local fly/tackle shop or call toll-free to order:
1-800-541-9498 (8-5 p.s.t.) • www.AmatoBooks.com

More Popular Books
from Frank Amato Publications

Tying & Fishing Soft-Hackled Nymphs
by Allen McGee

Soft-hackled nymphs imitate movement and behavior, pairing them with the most effective techniques brings these flies to life. These wingless wet flies provide you with unlimited presentation possibilities, and will bring more trout to your line.
8 1/2 x 11 inches, 96 pages, all color.

SB: $24.95
ISBN-13: 978-1-57188-403-9
UPC: 0-81127-00237-5

Morris & Chan on Fly Fishing Trout Lakes
by Skip Morris & Brian Chan

With the teaming of Skip Morris and Brian Chan, you are getting the advice of top experts in the fields of fly-fishing, fly-tying, entomology, and fish biology. This is your guide for improving and perfecting your skills as a lake fly-fisher. All-color, 8 1/2 x 11 inches, 96 pages.

SB: $24.95
ISBN-13: 978-1-57188-181-6
UPC: 0-66066-00392-8
HB: $39.95
ISBN-13: 978-1-57188-182-3
UPC: 0-66066-00393-5

Basic Stream Flies: How to Choose, Fish & Tie Them
by Jim Schollmeyer & Tracy Peterson

Basic Stream Flies will help you choose the right fly, when to fish it, where to fish it, and how. 28 fly patterns, including nymphs, emergers, dry flies, and streamers. Each pattern has a fly plate, photograph of the natural, the recipe, three useful variations, and tying steps. Fishing techniques are shown with clear illustrations and concise text. Chapters on water types, stream insects, terrestrials, leeches, and baitfish round out this informative book. 6 x 9 inches, 143 pages, all-color.

Spiral SB: $24.95
ISBN-13: 978-1-57188-436-7
UPC: 0-81127-00270-2

Ask for these books at your local fly/tackle shop or call toll-free to order:
1-800-541-9498 (8-5 p.s.t.) • www.AmatoBooks.com